MAKE ANYTHING HAPPEN

A Creative Guide to Vision Boards,
Goal Setting, and Achieving
the Life of Your Dreams

T0001426

CARRIE LINDSEY

Skyhorse Publishing

Copyright © 2018 by Carrie Lindsey

All rights reserved. No part of this book may be reproduced in any manner without the express written consent of the publisher, except in the case of brief excerpts in critical reviews or articles. All inquiries should be addressed to Skyhorse Publishing, 307 West 36th Street, 11th Floor, New York, NY 10018.

Skyhorse Publishing books may be purchased in bulk at special discounts for sales promotion, corporate gifts, fund-raising, or educational purposes. Special editions can also be created to specifications. For details, contact the Special Sales Department, Skyhorse Publishing, 307 West 36th Street, 11th Floor, New York, NY 10018 or info@skyhorsepublishing.com.

Skyhorse® and Skyhorse Publishing® are registered trademarks of Skyhorse Publishing, Inc.®, a Delaware corporation.

Visit our website at www.skyhorsepublishing.com.

10 9 8 7 6 5 4 3

Library of Congress Cataloging-in-Publication Data is available on file.

Cover design and image by Carrie Lindsey

Print ISBN: 978-1-5107-3414-2
Ebook ISBN: 978-1-5107-3415-9

Printed in China

contents

ritude is everything

UGH SHE BE
UT LITTLE,
HE IS FIERCE.

do what
you love
&
ove what
you do.

find something
to be grateful
for every day

GROW
this business x2

py day oh h

24

Part 1

Define Your Dreams

What Inspires You?

When I was a kid, I had a vision board. Tons of them, really. In fact, my entire bedroom was a vision board. Of course, at the time, I didn't have a word for it. I thought I was just obsessed with horses and liked putting pictures of them everywhere.

A couple of weeks ago, I pulled out a notebook that was in a box of junk from my childhood that my mom brought over one day. It was an old blue three-ring binder with a horse decal on the front.

Inside, divided into sections by color (bay, gray, paint) and discipline (English, western, dressage), were pages and pages of collages of horse pictures I particularly loved and cut out of magazines, and then glued onto pages that I collected in the binder.

If you had seen my room at the time, you would have seen almost every inch covered in horse posters.

I was going to work with horses when I grew up, and that was all there was to it.

"Wow," said my husband, Charles. "You were basically making vision boards when you were eight years old."

And, you guys, I totally was! I obviously didn't know it at the time, but I was putting my dreams onto paper and telling the universe that this is exactly what I was going to do, and I wasn't taking no for an answer.

I also wrote a ton, and even as a child, I knew I'd grow up to be an author. I just didn't know what I would write about. Well, when I was a kid I was pretty sure I'd grow up to write the next great American novel about horses, but by the time I had graduated from high school I realized I might be better with nonfiction (based on the eight thousand horse stories I started to write but never could find a way to wrap up).

For more than thirty years, I've known in my heart that I would write a book.

On my thirty-ninth birthday, I said to my husband, "This is the year I'm going to write my book." And shortly after that, I wrote, "Write a book" on my vision board.

As I sit here today, writing my book, I want you to know that it can be done. Whatever it is you want to do, you can do it. I want you to believe in yourself, I want you to get things done, and I want you to have fun doing it. I'm going to share some amazing tools for pinpointing your goals through vision boards and other creative outlets, and we're going to talk about exactly how to turn those goals into realized dreams.

First, you need to know what it is you're really trying to accomplish. *Your goals need to be defined.*

Second, you must give these goals some love and energy and really understand how it will look and feel when you accomplish them. *You need to visualize how it will be when you reach your goals.*

Finally, you can't ever rely on big dreams and wishful thinking when you want to make things happen. You have to take ownership of your goals, put solid plans into place, and work hard to see them through. *You need to implement plans and know how to follow through.*

Those are the things I'm going to help you with. Together, we'll define your goals. We'll visualize your success through some super fun exercises (vision boards!). And finally, we'll pull together strategies that will help you reach your goals.

Get ready to Make Anything Happen!

But wait! Before we *actually* get started, I have some resources I want to share with you.

Zig Ziglar once said, "People often say that motivation doesn't last. Well, neither does bathing—that's why we recommend it daily."

As someone who loves to read personal development books and inspirational stories—there are so many to be inspired by, y'all—this quote sticks with me. It's true—we need to be inspired daily. Inspiration can come in many forms.

In my life, I often find inspiration in a good book, a random article that pops up in my Facebook feed, a day outdoors with my horse. You'll find inspiration in places that are meaningful to you.

We're going to focus on the Inner Creative hiding inside you, just waiting to come out and sprinkle the world with your amazing ideas. We're going to focus on the Inner Doer, the one who, in my case, lies dormant most of the time because it's hard work to put those ideas into practice!

I believe you can reach your goals. I believe you can live the life of your dreams. I believe you are here for a reason.

Not to sound cheesy, but . . . I want this book to make you feel inspired, capable, and ready to *get things done.*

But if you're feeling stuck, I hope you'll join us in our private Make Anything Happen Facebook group. In this group, we encourage each other as we work toward our goals. I'm always posting actionable content and challenges (because being inspired is nice and all, but sorry—it won't make things happen for you) and sharing exclusive content. Throughout this book you'll find links and QR codes that lead to helpful bonus content (articles and printables) that I think you will like.

I'd also love to have you visit me at my blog, CarrieElle.com. I am constantly updating it with planning, vision boarding, and goal-setting content, including free printables and digital downloads designed to help you dream big, put an action plan in place, and reach those goals!

I'm so excited to start this journey with you. Let's get started, shall we?

Let's Talk About Priorities

To say I was obsessed with horses as a kid would be a huge understatement. Horses were my *life*, and that was before I ever took a riding lesson or owned a horse of my own.

Horses were everything to me.

When I was eight years old, I started taking riding lessons. When I got older, my jobs revolved around horses. Imagine being paid to do what your soul craves, every single day. It was as awesome as it sounds.

Eventually, I got married and moved to Texas with my husband, our dog and cat, and two horses.

As I fell into Texas life, and soon enough a job in the corporate world, the horses were still there, even though I no longer rode as often as I had in California.

This was okay, though. It was a busy season of my life, and I still had my horse (and two newly acquired mini donkeys). Soon enough, we had kids and moved to the suburbs.

It might sound like I gave up, but that wasn't it at all. I was following instincts that felt right at the time. Adjusting to motherhood was tough. I needed to focus on one thing at a time, and for me, that meant that horses fell to the wayside for a while.

I'll never forget some wise advice I had when I was pregnant with my son, super busy with my job, and worried that I'd never ride again.

"Horses will always be there," someone told me. It was hard to believe, but guess what? She was right! Horses did not go extinct in the years I spent raising my babies.

My kids are older now, and a year ago, I noticed myself *really* missing my horse. The "old me" that lived at the barn, loved to get dirty, and found joy watching her horse munch on a carrot had been lying dormant for years. But she was still there, just waiting for the right time to magically reappear when she'd have spare money (horses are expensive) and extra hours at her beck and call.

Are you following me here?

I thought *things would get easy and I'd suddenly have all the resources I needed* to start riding again (such as money to afford an expensive board bill at a local barn and free time to ride every day).

If I sat around waiting for the "right" time to come, I would never again see my horse.

The truth is, I needed a little break from horses to focus on my family and my job. That was totally okay. But when that little voice inside me reminded me that I was ready to reclaim that part of my life, I was tempted to ignore it, because acknowledging it would mean I'd have to put in some work.

See, when we moved to the suburbs, we moved my horse into a family member's barn. He was an hour away from me, living in a big pasture, with no arena to ride in. Board was affordable and care was good. It was the perfect scenario for the horse.

But having to drive an hour each way to see him wasn't a perfect scenario for me.

For years (literally), I waited until "things settled down" and I won the lottery, so I could afford to move him to a barn nearby.

Well, guess what? Things never settled down. *They got busier.* And I *still* haven't won the lottery.

At some point, my valid reasons for not going to visit him turned into nothing more than lame excuses.

I wasn't making horses a priority.

The truth is not that I didn't have time. It's that I didn't want to *make* time.

And that is how I define a priority. A priority is something so important to you, you make time to do it.

And so this year, I made horses a priority.

I found a local therapeutic riding center and I started volunteering a few hours a week. I can't even tell you the joy this brought me. As I pulled away from the barn every Friday afternoon, after a morning of twirling manes between my fingers and organizing bridles in a dusty tack room, I felt a centered peace that I hadn't realized was missing.

Suddenly, the trivial problems in my life seemed manageable and insignificant. Spending time with horses put me back in touch with *me*.

My horse is still an hour away. It's truly not realistic for me to go see him every day. But once a week? *Certainly.*

I take my kids and, every week, we make a day of it.

And guess what? When I focus on my priorities—the real priorities, that I feel in my bones—everything else falls into place, too. It's a crazy thing.

Somehow, forcing myself to take a half day and drive across Texas to get dirty and teach the kids to ride and watch the horses munch on carrots has spilled over into being more productive for the rest of my week.

So. Let's talk about *your* priorities.

Priorities can change. That's normal, and that's okay.

A priority is something that is *important to you, that might require you to sacrifice in other areas, and that ultimately has a huge payoff* (even if you can't see it right now).

Getting groceries each week so we stay on track with healthy eating? *A priority.*

Spending a few hours each week working on our budget so we understand our finances? *A priority.*

Carving out four to five hours each week to take the kids to visit the horses? *A priority.*

Cleaning my house every day? *Not a priority.* But it might be a priority in YOUR life, and if that is the case, I am jealous.

Staying true to my priorities makes me feel centered and on track.

Ultimately, my priorities feed into my goals. Some of these goals—like creating a new product for my shop—are tangible, measurable, and something I'm held accountable for by others.

Other goals, like living a life well-lived and pursuing joy every chance I get, aren't as measurable—but they're just as important.

In order to live the life I want to live, in order to create the products I set out to create, I have to keep one thing in my sights—my priorities.

It's a funny thing, priorities. As important as they are, it's awfully easy to let them slip.

Later, we're going to talk about goals and planning strategies and *making things happen.*

But, first, we need to promise ourselves to remain true to our inner selves. And that means *we need to know and honor our priorities.*

Let's play a little game! It's easy, I promise—there is no wrong way to play.

In the space below on the next page, sketch out your priorities. This could be a literal sketch (I still love doodling horse pictures), or you could just write them down (no bonus points for cute handwriting, but if I had cute handwriting, I'd totally go for it). You might want to cut pictures out of magazines that say it best, or print out some of your favorite photos and stick them here. Be creative and have fun with it. Your priorities should be sparkling beacons of joy in your life, and this page represents that!

Take a look at some of my own if you need to get the juices flowing (yours may look similar to or nothing like mine). Remember that your priorities are The Most Important Thing to you. Also, remember that they can change. Mine have, many times.

I use my priorities as a guideline for how well I'm living. If I am, indeed, making these things a priority, I'm doing okay, and everything else sort of settles into place.

My Priorities:

My favorite things

What Does Your Best Life Look Like?

Let's talk about our dream lives for a minute (this is my favorite part).

Your best life.

What does your Best Life look like?

It will look different for every person. Your best life will look different from *my* best life.

My Best Life includes miniature donkeys living in my backyard. *Yours may not* (and your neighbors will thank you for it, trust me).

Also? Your Best Life might change. It's okay to want one thing now and later realize you actually don't want that one thing at all. Or, maybe you have it and then move on to something else.

It's okay for it to change. We all change, and it's important to give yourself permission to change.

When I was a kid, I knew that I'd grow up to be a horse trainer. I'd teach riding lessons and have my own farm and breed show ponies.

It never, for one second, occurred to me that I might not actually do this.

As it turned out, I did grow up to teach riding lessons. For several years, I taught lessons as a certified therapeutic riding instructor and also traveled to local homes to teach people to ride.

I was living my best life.

One of the reasons we moved to Texas, in fact, was because I wanted to have horse property.

We sold our little condo in southern California and moved to rural Texas, where we had land and horses and a barn and even a lighted arena! *I was living my best life.*

But guess what?

Our lives changed. I got a "normal" job (and I loved it). We had kids. And suddenly, I wasn't so interested in being a horse trainer and raising show ponies anymore. It was all I could do to raise my own, two-legged spawn, let alone a barn full of fancy horses!

My Best Life changed. And that was totally okay. When I felt the pendulum start to swing, I embraced it. We moved to the suburbs. We bought a house in a neighborhood full of children, walking trails, and playgrounds. *And we loved it.*

Six years later, though, I feel the pendulum swinging again. As the kids get older, I feel changes on the horizon and my Best Life vision takes on new shape. I embrace the changes.

Here are some examples of what my best life looks like today:

- Miniature donkeys in my backyard
- Energy and health for myself and my family
- A thriving business that supports my family financially and gives back to our community
- A room full of books
- Summer trips to Oregon with my family
- Consistent yoga practice
- Peace within

You'll notice that some of these things are material (a room full of books). Others are not ("peace within" is pretty vague, but it has meaning to me).

Again, there is no right or wrong way to define the life you want to live.

What does *your* Best Life look like? Use the space on the next page to jot down or doodle your visions, your dreams, your best life. You can also cut out magazine pictures to depict the things that are important to you (but don't forget, magazine pictures are staged and edited, not representative of "real life" for anyone).

Check back in on these pages whenever you need to remember what it is you're working toward.

Set Yourself Up for Success

So, you have a business you want to start or a place you want to visit or a million dollars you want to make (or all three, yay!). Now what?

Maybe you need some help—some motivation or inspiration to sit down and finally get to it. I'm going to walk you through what I do when I'm feeling completely overwhelmed by all the ideas (or all the work) and find myself procrastinating.

I am a horrible housekeeper. This is the truth. But even though I'm not great at housekeeping—understatement alert!—I love having a clean house. I thrive in a clean house. This is especially true in my office.

I've created a work space I love and I encourage you to do the same. If you don't have a personal work space, do what you can with what you've got. Make your laptop cute—have you seen those adorable keypad stickers? Get a pretty notebook and a nice pen. Have your favorite mug nearby. Just little things that make you feel good about your space.

Next, clean that space.

Whenever I don't know where to start, I start with cleaning my desk. If you follow me on Instagram, I'm always sharing before-and-after pictures of my work space because I live in a cycle of cluttered to clean and back to cluttered again all week long.

> Whenever I don't know where to start, I start with cleaning my desk.

When it's time to work (and this can be work on my laptop, a marathon cleaning session, or even working out), the first thing I do, if I want to be truly productive, is to get rid of all my distractions. I put my phone on airplane mode (you can turn the volume off, but I find that I mindlessly pick up my phone and check social media without thinking about it—when my phone's in airplane mode and I pick it up, it reminds me that I'm wasting time and to get back to it). I close my email and all social media on my laptop and set a timer (usually for an hour).

I always have a notebook (or ten) nearby, and, if I get stuck, I'll start working on a brain dump in my notebook. Sometimes, I'll even use this time to decorate my journal or my planner. I've found that this kind of creative work, while perhaps not directly related to what I'm supposed to be doing, is a great way to get the creative juices flowing and often surprises me by spurring ideas that relate to what I should be doing. It's important that I keep this hour free of outside distractions and dedicate myself to getting my work done while I can.

When I get really stuck, I go outside. Sometimes I take a walk around the block, but usually just sitting on the front porch and breathing in some fresh air is enough to free up whatever it is that's blocking me creatively. Even if I don't come back to my desk with a new idea, I come back with fresh air in my lungs, and I strongly believe in the good that comes from fresh air.

I've also learned that taking care of myself is important, and not just for the obvious reasons. When I eat well, exercise, and get enough sleep, I have a clearer head. I have more energy, and it's easier to work on big projects and tap into my creativity when I am feeling my best. And even though I'd literally eat donuts and read books all day if I could, I feel best when I eat a clean diet, get outside, work out, and sleep.

It takes me forever to fall asleep, so I've learned to shut down all social media well before bedtime. I feel like staying off social media before bed is a good thing to do emotionally, but staying away from the blue light of our phones is important if we are to fall asleep. My laptop also has an application installed called f.lux—this warms the blue light of my laptop the later in the evening it gets, which helps my body prepare for sleep (you can always disable it if you need to).

When I'm feeling *really* stuck, I'll just walk away from it. This is when I find myself taking a day off to go see my horse. I come back feeling centered, refreshed, and usually ready to tackle whatever it was I was struggling with.

Find what centers you—working out, reading a book, ice-skating—and always go back to that when you're really stuck. In fact, I've learned that going back to what I know is a great way to get the creative juices flowing and give me a little boost of confidence when I need it most.

How to Find More Time

I bet you're like me when it comes to time—you never have enough.

Time is the same for everyone. It's what we *do* with our time that really matters. I like to procrastinate as much as the next person (maybe more), and it's a constant battle to stay on track and own my time (rather than letting it own me). I want to share with you some tricks I employ every day to help me manage my time better. You'll be amazed at how much you can get done when you take advantage of all the time you are given.

Outsource—pay someone else to do things you don't need to do. We've hired a housekeeper before to help around the house. I'll pay a few dollars more to have my groceries delivered. There are also dinner delivery services that will bring fresh, healthy meals to your doorstep, ready to be cooked. If you're starting a new business or really need to get some serious, uninterrupted hours in and you have kids, consider hiring someone to help with child care.

It can be hard to hand over the money when money is tight, but if you could be making more money or getting more done doing a job that only you can do—like starting your business, creating a new product, or decorating your master bedroom—consider the value of hiring someone to fill in the spots you can't fill at that moment.

Meal plan. Meal planning will reduce stress and chaos in your life, help you eat healthier, and save you money. I have an entire course on meal planning that you can take for free (www.carrieelle.com/30-day-meal-plan-challenge). The short version, though, is to grab a piece of paper, fill in your evening activities (like "soccer," "date night," etc.), and then plan a meal for each night. On the same paper, write out your grocery list as you're writing out your menu. It will take you fifteen or twenty minutes and save much more time than that. Bonus if you do some meal prep, too!

Meal planning can apply to all meals or just to dinner. If you know your mornings are crazy, spend an hour on the weekend prepping breakfasts that you can grab and go. I've found that the better I feel, the more likely I am to get things done, and that means taking care of myself and making sure I'm eating well.

Get down to inbox zero. I'm an inbox zero girl. Not my stack-of-papers-next-to-me inbox, but my email inbox. I make sure I deal with every email I receive, and the best way to do that is to get down to inbox zero as often as possible. The crazy thing about emails is that they seem to spring from seemingly nowhere. Ever wonder how you ended up on a list you are certain you never signed up for? Companies are selling your email address every day.

The junk mail I get every day is ridiculous, and I can think of hundreds of better uses of my time than deleting junk mail from my inbox. I use an email program called Unroll.me to organize my emails. There are lots of programs like this out there—I use the free version of Unroll.me. This service lets you "roll up" your emails into one daily digest or unsubscribe from them in one simple dashboard. All of those email lists you don't like to see every day, but won't unsubscribe from because every now and then they send you something important? Roll 'em up.

Every day, I scroll through my daily digest of my rolled-up emails. Every few days, I go to the dashboard and unsubscribe from all the email lists I don't

You know what's super important? Sleep!

want to be on (I almost never subscribe to email lists, but I find that I get added to several every day!).

If you're overwhelmed, just go by letter. On day one, unsubscribe or roll up all of your emails that start with "A." It took me about a week to initially get my emails all cleaned up, but now I go in every few days and, starting at "A," go through and clean up my list a few email addresses at a time.

The amount of email I'm receiving is probably a third of what it used to be. I still have to stay on top of it, but it's much easier than spending fifteen minutes every day just hitting the "delete" button.

Also, clearing my emails out to inbox zero means that I'm actually keeping up with my emails.

For the emails I do receive (and that don't get rolled up), I address the email and then file it into a folder.

Turn off your phone at night. You know what's super important? Sleep! It's taken me years (and two kids) to take sleep seriously, but now I realize that a good night's sleep can make all the difference in the world. Sleep has always been hard for me—it seems like laying my head down on my pillow is an invitation for every item on my to-do list, every stressor of my day, every worry I can think up, and every great idea to pop into my head. Add to that my phone dinging at 1:00 a.m. when my friends two time zones away start group texting me, and it can be almost impossible to sleep (I like to pay them back by responding to all their texts first thing in the morning).

I actually like to put my phone in airplane mode at night. That way, I'm not as tempted to grab it and aimlessly scroll through Instagram. And of course, no calls or texts go through. My husband leaves his phone on, and I know that if a family member needs to reach me for an emergency, they can call him.

When I'm traveling or if I want to leave my phone on for certain people, I change the settings so only calls or texts from those people come through. I only learned about this cool trick a while ago, and I want to make sure you know about it too, because those random texts in the middle of the night can really do a number on your sleep and *ain't nobody got time for that.*

Use a timer. Set a timer when you work, and while that timer is ticking down, make sure you're actually working. Turn off the social media. Close your email. Turn off your phone. Use that time to do one thing, and do it well.

You can also use a timer to remind yourself to get up and stretch if you sit at a computer all day. You can use it to motivate yourself to do little chores around the house (set it for fifteen minutes and see how much of the linen closet you can organize in that time). Timers are great for working out, too—doing a workout every day might seem daunting, but if you tell yourself you only have to work out for twenty minutes, it's not so bad. The timer will also keep you honest—it will go off when the time is done, and not before!

Keep your priorities front and center. Whenever I feel a little crazy with all the stuff in my life, I bring it back to my priorities. Specifically, my life priorities—my kids, my goals, the trip I want to take. On busy workdays, I bring it back to that one thing I need to do, and I focus on that until it's done.

Try using an hourly day planner. I find the structure of an hourly planner too limiting. It stresses me out and makes me feel like a failure when I don't stick to my day exactly like I wrote it down. My days are fluid and almost never go exactly as planned, and an hourly schedule feels rigid and sets me up for disappointment because I can almost never stick to it.

Some people thrive with a structured calendar like this, though, and if you're one of those people I encourage you to keep using this system.

I also encourage everyone struggling to find time in their day to use an hourly system for a week to track their activities. Once you have to write down, "9 a.m.: Wasted an hour on Facebook," my guess is you'll be much more cognizant of the time you're spending on social media!

If you can't find any extra time in your day to spend on the things that are important to you, try this exercise for a week—I bet you'll find that time after all.

Cut the Fat

Okay, so now we have established what makes us tick and keeps us centered. Why is it, then, that it's so easy to get distracted and fall off track? If our priorities are so important to us, why do we stray from them?

Why do I let myself get swept up in the whirlwind of life and complain about how I don't have the time to visit my horse, to work out, to sit down and do homework with the kids?

I believe most of us really need to cut the fat.

That is especially true in my own life. I am always trying to figure out what I can *stop* doing so I can spend more time doing the things that I love.

Case in point: laundry.

I don't love laundry. I don't *mind* laundry, but I certainly don't love it.

Yesterday, I was totally stressed out. Like, super stressed. And I was cleaning at the same time. Actually, I was stressed about cleaning. There was so much to do, and so little time. I found myself wishing, not for the first time, that I could just be one of those people who clean for stress relief. Seriously, why can't I be that person? But I'm not, so my solution is to keep working hard until I can afford a cleaning service. And then I won't have a dirty house to stress about in the first place, and all will be well.

Back to the laundry.

I read a book (maybe you have read it, too) called *The Life-Changing Magic of Tidying Up*, by Marie Kondo. I actually found this book to be very helpful. The short version is, you pick items up in your house, and if it brings you joy—real joy!—you keep it. If it doesn't bring you joy, you get rid of it, because *life is too short for clutter you don't like.*

There are many, many things we do in our lives that we don't need to do.

I had a hard time applying the rules to my kids, though. You see, what brings my kids joy most certainly does *not* bring me joy (if I find one more Pokémon card in my bathroom . . .).

What I did find I could apply, though, was her joyous way of folding laundry (stay with me!).

I do the laundry. And until recently, I also put all the laundry away.

I would joyfully fold up my kids' laundry using the method described in the book (so neat! Such pretty little lines of folded shirts in their dressers, like happy little soldiers ready for their day!). I even folded their underwear, y'all.

And then, approximately three minutes and seven seconds later, one of the kids would need a shirt and they'd start pulling out my beautifully folded masterpieces and tossing them back into the drawers helter-skelter.

Ugh!

I tried showing them my method. I tried asking them to just take one shirt out at a time. I tried making them put the shirts back.

But you know what? Nicely folding laundry for my kids wasn't worth it. It was taking time away from others things I could be doing. So I bought two laundry baskets—one for each kid. And instead of putting their folded laundry away, I quit folding it completely. I pull it out of the dryer, toss it in the appropriate basket, and tell them to put it away in the proper drawers however they please, so long as they put it away.

One day I realized I was fighting a joyless, losing battle, so I just up and quit folding my kids' laundry, although I still fold my own clothes the joyful way. It really did happen just like that, too.

And what a relief!

There are many, many things we do in our lives that we don't need to do. These time-wasters take away from the things we want to be doing.

Let's cut the fat!

Here are some time-wasters you might be engaging in. Does any of this sound familiar?

- Folding your kids' laundry when they are just going to destroy it anyway (booo, kids!)

- Checking Facebook or email ten times (or more) a day

- Hitting the snooze button more than once (or twice, or three times, or, well, you get the idea!)

- TV

- Saying yes to things we really don't want or need to do

When we cut out the nonsense, we're able to live more intentionally. Instead of spending hours checking social media (and all those times you check Instagram "for just a minute" add up to hours, trust me) or following through on commitments we wish we hadn't committed to, we're able to do the things that are actually important to us. *The things that can actually impact our lives in a positive manner.*

Cutting the fat can give you hours—yes, hours—of "extra" time each week. Think of what you could do with extra *hours*, y'all.

Here are some ways I cut the fat:

- I quit folding my kids' laundry (whew!).

- I rarely watch TV during the week (I try to keep my movie-watching and Netflix bingeing to the weekends).

- Limit social media (I don't do social media at night or first thing in the morning, either).

- SAY NO. Y'all. I probably get ten to twenty emails a day from people wanting something from me (usually, they want coverage on my blog). And that's not to mention the regular, day-to-day requests (volunteering at the kids' school, bringing snacks to soccer games, etc.). I am very intentional with my time. I don't do things I don't want to do anymore.

Let's talk about all the things you could get rid of to make time for your priorities. Could you shut off your phone earlier at night? Watch less TV? Say no more often? Hire a housekeeper (that's next on my list)?

Use the space on the next page to identify your time-wasters. The important thing here is just that you are identifying and acknowledging the ways you waste time. Don't feel bad. We all do it. I'd even say I'm a Time Wasting Queen. It's something I am always working on!

Once you've identified where your "extra" time is going, you'll be able to recapture it and use it more productively, even if that means turning off the TV earlier and using your extra time to get more sleep.

Part II

Visualize Your End Game

#Goals

If you're reading this book, it's likely because you want to make something happen.

Maybe you have a product you want to create. Maybe you'd like to lose ten pounds and can't seem to find the motivation. Maybe you want to design a beautiful home but feel overwhelmed by all the steps to get you from "idea" to "finished product."

You have *goals*.

A while back, my daughter, who was five at the time, wanted to make a craft. I pulled out a box of random crafting supplies and told her to have at it.

Before I knew it, she'd dug out a huge collection of loose pom-poms that were scattered throughout the box.

"I don't know how I'm going to make a fox, but I know I'm going to make it," she told me, determinedly holding up a handful of multicolored pom-poms.

How profound, I thought. *She basically just summed up my entire creative process in one sentence.* I don't know *how* I'm going to get something done, but I know I'm going to do it.

What Claire was telling me was basically a metaphor for many of the goals I've had in my life. Some of them seemed impossible at the time. Some of them still do!

Despite the questionable path to achieve my goals, I've always believed that I *can* achieve them. I just need to know what they *are*, so I can get started chipping away at them and turning them into a reality.

The first step to getting things done is defining exactly what needs to be done.

In this case, Claire needed to make a fox.

From there, it was a matter of collecting the proper tools (glue, pom-poms, and googly eyes), putting a process in place (glue this to that, and that to this), and working on it until there was a fox.

Making a fox out of pom-poms is no easy task. I mean, have you seen fox ears? They're pointy. Have you seen a pom-pom? They are not pointy. But Claire was determined, and she knew *exactly* what she wanted, and that is a great place to start.

Merriam-Webster defines goal as *"the end toward which effort is directed"*.

In Claire's case, the "end" was a fox. The effort was directed through collecting everything she needed and putting it together.

We're going to talk a lot about putting effort into things.

But right now, I want you to think about the end results.

What is your end game?

What, *specifically*, do you want to accomplish?

Your priorities are clear. Your Best Life has been defined. Now, how do we make your Best Life a reality while keeping your priorities straight?

That, my friend, is what we're going to start working on next. *This is the fun part!*

Let's start with one goal.

Think about it. Pick one goal. Maybe it's simple, like losing five pounds. Or maybe it's something big, so big, you're even a little bit afraid to think about it, let alone say it out loud. That's okay. *Those are the best ones.*

This book, you guys? This book is exactly the kind of goal I was afraid to admit—to myself, and certainly out loud—when I first felt it forming in my mind.

You see, I knew I wanted to be an author from sometime around 1984 when I realized authors were a thing. I never stopped thinking I could be an author, but as I got older it became less clear how that would happen. Then, in 2011, I decided to get serious about my blog. At that point, I knew, again, that I wanted to write a book.

I just didn't know what that would look like. And I was embarrassed to tell anyone I wanted to write a book, because *who was I, anyway*?

Does any of this sound familiar?

I didn't feel qualified to write a book. I didn't admit to anyone that my dream was to write a book. But I kept it inside, never ignoring the tug I felt in my heart whenever I thought about it, and I did the only thing I knew to move toward my goal.

I wrote.

I nurtured the growth of my blog. I got better at creating content. I learned to take pictures. I worked hard, and I was consistent. I never lost sight of my goal, even when I was unsure about how I'd ever get there.

And guess what, y'all?

I'm writing a book.

Not only am I writing a book, but in the last year, it's become clear exactly what I should write about—I literally have a list of books I can't wait to write!

This story is important to share with you guys, because it illustrates how I took something that was deeply true to me—wanting to write a book—and plugged away, slowly and surely over the years, until it became my reality.

Some goals can be reached in a short amount of time (that five pounds you want to lose? I bet you can do it in a few weeks!). Others take time.

We're in it for the long haul, here.

Let's talk about *your* goals.

Go ahead and pick a few goals. Mix it up a little—pick some short-term, easy-to-accomplish goals, and pick some Big Scary goals. You don't have to share these with anyone. You just need to be honest with yourself about what they are.

Use the space on the following pages to define your goals.

One more thing, though. Don't just put your goals in this space.

I want you to say them out loud. Don't say, "I wish I could write a book." Instead, say, "I am going to write a book." Don't say, "I need to lose five pounds." Say, "I am going to lose five pounds." Say it with conviction. It will feel good, I promise.

DREAM BIG
goal trackers

Goal	Goal	Goal	Goal
ACTION ITEMS	ACTION ITEMS	ACTION ITEMS	ACTION ITEMS

NOTES	NOTES	NOTES	NOTES
DUE DATE	DUE DATE	DUE DATE	DUE DATE
Accomplished ☐	Accomplished ☐	Accomplished ☐	Accomplished ☐

DREAM BIG
goal trackers

Goal	Goal	Goal	Goal
ACTION ITEMS	ACTION ITEMS	ACTION ITEMS	ACTION ITEMS
_____	_____	_____	_____
_____	_____	_____	_____
_____	_____	_____	_____
_____	_____	_____	_____
_____	_____	_____	_____
_____	_____	_____	_____
_____	_____	_____	_____
_____	_____	_____	_____
_____	_____	_____	_____
_____	_____	_____	_____
_____	_____	_____	_____
_____	_____	_____	_____
NOTES	NOTES	NOTES	NOTES
DUE DATE	DUE DATE	DUE DATE	DUE DATE
Accomplished ☐	Accomplished ☐	Accomplished ☐	Accomplished ☐

Manifesting Your Destiny

My husband, Charles, and I run our own small business. I design planners, and together we sell them. This means that I handle the blogging, the designing, and the social media, while Charles handles all of the logistics—this includes working with vendors, printing and order fulfillment, and everything technical.

I work from home 99 percent of the time, while Charles works at the shop 99 percent of the time.

It wasn't always like this! We used to work exclusively from home. This business was built in our master bedroom, on a little home printer. Then two home printers, then three. We eventually outgrew our space at home, rented a little office space, and outsourced our printing needs to a "real" printer.

As we continued to grow, though, it became apparent that we could save money by bringing printing back in house. (That was quite a conundrum. We loved the flexibility and the quality of the products we could print using a real printer, but it was so expensive!) It was hard to know when to bring it all back in house, but eventually we started purchasing equipment that would let us create most of our products in our own work space.

One of our most popular products is a Meal Planner. Each page has a perforated grocery list that you can rip off and take to the store with you. This is key to the product, but the perforation process was expensive and time-consuming because the pages had to be printed and then outsourced to someone who could perforate them.

WEEKLY MENU

Week of: September 18

18	crock pot sour cream chicken
19	hamburgers + sweet pot
20	chicken + salad
21	BLTs + fr
22	BBC

GROCERY LIST

produce
- spinach
- onions
- bananas
- zucchini

dairy
- sour cream
- cream cheese
- milk

bread
- buns

You guys. Printing equipment is expensive. Like, e-x-p-e-n-s-i-v-e. After purchasing a few key pieces, we realized that the next big piece we needed was a perforator. The way we decide which equipment to buy next is mostly based on what costs the most to have done, and, at this point, the perforation was the most expensive step.

This expense came right when we had the absolute least amount of flexibility possible, both time-wise and financially. It was summer, which is a super slow time for our business. We were already stretching every penny as far as we could. It also happened to be right when we ran out of Meal Planners and the daily emails started pouring in, asking when we'd have more.

We needed Meal Planners to sell so we could make money, but we needed money so we could buy the equipment to make the meal planners.

We decided that we needed to make this perforator happen *STAT*.

At the time, I was reading *You Are a Badass at Making Money* by Jen Sincero. Throughout the book, she talks about being open to money arriving when you need it or want it.

I'm sure many of you have had this happen before. You are completely broke and need to pay a bill, and the money magically appears. Or maybe you're getting married, and all of a sudden you notice wedding stuff is everywhere you look. You don't recall seeing it before you were engaged, but suddenly the billboards are full of engagement rings, the magazines bursting with ads for wedding registries, and the radio ablaze with ads for an upcoming bridal convention.

This kind of thing happens, and you're not imagining it—it's real!

So, as I was reading this book, I was super duper *extra* attentive to my current financial needs (which, as I've said, were plenty). In fact, I would often read passages to Charles, and I was constantly saying (sometimes in a not-so-serious way), "Let's manifest us some money!"

We simply did not have an extra $4,200 for a perforator, but we were going to have to find it somewhere.

One day, as I sat behind my laptop at home, Charles pinged me on Google Chat. "I found the perforator we need," he said (it was local). "We just need $4,200."

Five minutes later, he pings me again. This time he says, "I found the machine we need for $750."

$750!

We had recently purchased a cutting machine, and the idea popped into his head to call the guy who sold us the cutter and ask if he knew of any used perforators. Not only did he, but he had one in his barn that had arrived just yesterday, was an older version of the exact machine we needed, and was only $750.

Now, to be totally honest, even $750 was a huge stretch that month. But it was less of a stretch than $4,200, and I was celebrating this win.

"Now we only need to manifest $750 to pay for this thing!" I told Charles.

Not fifteen minutes later, the mail came. I got the mail, as I do, and noticed an envelope with unfamiliar handwriting on it. I opened it up, and lo and behold, it was a check for $690 from our old landlord. It was both earlier and more than we had expected, and it brought our total perforator deficit down to only sixty dollars.

Not twenty minutes after that, Charles called me and said he'd just completed a little print job for a local business. He was paid seventy dollars for the job.

I had goosebumps all over.

For days, I'd been focusing my attention on bringing in some much-needed money. For days, we'd been talking about pulling the trigger on the perforator. Then, in a matter of less than two hours, we found the machine we needed, for less money than we needed, and *almost the exact amount of money that we needed* rolled into our lives.

Just like that!

> Manifesting something is . . . dreaming about it and then working toward your goal with a creative and open mind, and a strong sense of purpose.

Now, I know it's not always like that. But, I am also 100 percent open to receiving money and committed to finding the Financial Meadow of Endless Dollars.

You got to commit, you know what I mean?

Being committed means I'm open to manifesting money in many different ways, and in many different forms. A dollar is a dollar is a dollar. Certainly, my favorite kind of money is the kind that just shows up unexpectedly. But it's not realistic to just sit around and wait for money to materialize.

I'm talking about money, but this is not a book about manifesting money. This is just an example I think we can all relate to.

I believe that we manifest the things we desire in many different ways. For example, if it's money I'm after (and it is! You hear that, Money?), I might find that I take extra jobs to meet my money desires. I might create a new product. I might start paying attention to money and letting my mind be more open and accepting to creative opportunities to earn (for example, responding to emails I might normally ignore because they seem like dead ends or junk mail, but which could possibly be a great opportunity). I might reach out to my website's ad providers and have them audit my site and restructure some of the ads, which in turn could lead to more money. I might sell some stuff. I might work harder on my budget.

I might invest in a perforator that will save us literally thousands of dollars over the next year.

All of these things nurture my money goals and, miraculously, help me to manifest exactly what I desire—in this case, money!

Manifesting something is not just dreaming about it, creating a vision board full of dollar signs, and then hoping for the best. It's dreaming about it and then working toward your goal with a creative and open mind, and a strong sense of purpose.

I know what some of you are thinking. You're thinking, "Yes! Let's do this!"

And I know what others are thinking. You're thinking, "Okay, weirdo, you've been lucky, but I don't believe this crap!"

So, I want to bring in some science to back me up.

You probably already know that athletes are often told to visualize their performance. You've seen athletes on TV wearing headphones and closing their eyes before a big game or a swim meet (I watch the Olympics, and I see the swimmers doing this all the time).

Here's a super interesting study that makes a strong case for visualization (which to me, is the basis of manifesting anything—you see it in your head, and then you make it happen).

Guang Ye, an exercise psychologist from Cleveland Clinic Foundation, compared two groups of people: one group who went to the gym and worked out, and another group who just worked out in their heads (sounds a little woo-woo, right?). Of course, the people who worked out increased their muscle mass, and by about 30 percent at that. But here's the kicker!

The people who just worked out in their heads, visualizing their workouts but not actually doing them, also gained muscle mass—at a whopping 13.5 percent.[1]

Y'all. They imagined their muscles getting stronger, spent a lot of time thinking about it, and then their muscles actually got stronger.

If you can imagine stronger muscles and then end up with stronger muscles, it stands to reason that you can imagine lots of things and end up with exactly those things.

---

1   Ranganathan, Vinoth K., Vlodek Siemionow, Jing Z. Liu, Vinod Sahgal, and Guang H. Yue. "From mental power to muscle power—gaining strength by using the mind." *Neuropsychologia* 42, no. 7 (2004): 944-56. doi:10.1016/j.neuropsychologia.2003.11.018.

Olympians routinely use imagery as part of their training programs. A sports psychologist for the U.S. Olympic team, Nicole Detling, says, "The more an athlete can imagine the entire package, the better it's going to be."

Athletes think about what they want, and they physically and mentally work to improve until they reach their highest levels of performance.

I think this is profound. Olympians imagine their entire performance, and they perform better. Random people imagine working out, and they get stronger.

This means that you and I and everyone else can tap into this phenomenon. We can all visualize things and then make them happen.

And what better way to do it than with a beautiful vision board and a solid plan of attack?

What Is a Vision Board, and Why Do I Need One?

A vision board is a tool that can help you define your goals and keep your eye on the prize, so to speak.

Usually, a vision board is a collection of images and words specifically chosen to direct your focus toward a particular goal you have in your life. These images can be displayed on a board where you can see them on a daily basis (although any type of "board" will do, as we'll discuss).

A vision board can be an elaborate collection of ideas, words, and pictures on a giant poster you hang on your wall, or it can be a mini version with just a few key pieces of information that you keep tucked away in your purse and pull out when you need to see it.

Basically, it can be as dramatic or as simple as you want it to be.

And while you may have seen claims that you can make a vision board and things will magically manifest in your life, I'm here to tell you that's not *quite* true.

You certainly might see some things manifest just by setting your intention (in fact, you likely will, and in magical ways), but don't be fooled into thinking all your dreams will just start coming true as soon as you've pieced together your vision board.

Sorry, but *you're going to have to put in the work*.

A vision board will help you clarify what it is you're working toward, though. It will give you something to focus on. It will inspire you. It will put you on the right track. You can have one, or you can have many. You can post it where everyone can see it, or you can hide it away for your eyes only.

As a bonus, they're super fun to make.

And one more thing.

Vision boards don't make you "weird." Spending hours crafting a beautiful vision board doesn't mean you've gone off the deep end or that you're about to join a cult.

Vision boards are not just a bunch of bunk, and here are some reasons why you need to get on board.

Have you ever seen a graphic designer compile a board full of ideas and inspiration for a room she's about to decorate? (If not, spend a couple of hours on HGTV and I'm pretty sure you'll see what I mean!)

Have you ever seen a boss sketch out annual company goals on a whiteboard?

Have you ever taken a yoga class where the instructor asked you to "set your intention" at the beginning of the class?

These are all basically the same thing. Someone has taken their vision for a finished product, defined it, and made it real before it's actually real.

The designer knows exactly what colors and prints she wants to use, the boss (and anyone who sees the whiteboard) knows the company's financial goals, and the yoga students know what is important to them at that moment.

Don't lose sight of what a vision board really is—a place to envision your goals as you want them to be realized.

When you know what colors you want your finished room to be, you're hyperaware of those colors and find beautiful products in those exact shades, even when you aren't necessarily looking. You don't get distracted by all the other colors, because you know what colors you're seeking.

When you define your financial goals and put them out there for all the employees to see, the entire company keeps those numbers in the back of their head as they make sales calls, deal with customers, and make plans for growth.

When you set your intention as "flexibility" before your yoga practice, you find room to stretch into your poses you might not have had last week. Invariably, you take that flexibility mind-set with you throughout the day (yoga's not just about working out, y'all).

A vision board is the same thing—but it's tailored 100 percent to you, your dreams, and your life.

I'm going to teach you how to make your vision boards fun, pretty to look at (if that's what floats your boat), and super functional. But don't lose sight of what a vision board really is—*a place to envision your goals as you want them to be realized.*

Because vision boards are so flexible and so personal, they come in many shapes and forms! You can literally go and start doodling/cutting pictures out of magazines/printing inspirational quotes off the Internet right this second and get that vision board going.

I feel like many people get stuck on the ideas of vision boards because they think they just aren't creative, but that's not true.

You are creative. And your vision board doesn't *need* to be beautiful—it needs to be functional. It needs to remind you of your goals and give you a place to focus.

If you like to scrapbook, work in a planner, or keep a journal—you've already got a place to put your vision board. You most certainly do not need to hang it where everyone can see it (although being able to access it and check in with it every now and then are important, so make sure you put it somewhere that you'll see it often).

If you feel intimidated by the process of creating a vision board from scratch, I have some resources for you!

Not sure where to start? Scan the QR code for vision board templates (be inspired or straight-up print these templates out and use them for your own boards).

Want to make it cute? Print out these quotes and artwork to dress up your boards.

Here are some other tips to help you jump-start the process of making your vision board:

- If you don't know where to start, start with your Best Life. Make a vision board of what your Best Life looks like. Then, pick one of the goals on that board and create a vision board just for that goal.

- If you want a cute, personalized look but can't draw and suck at hand lettering (it's okay, I suck at hand lettering, too), find some cute fonts and print out the words you want to write. You can also print out coloring pages that you can color (anybody can color!), cut up, and add to your board.

- Cut up your old magazines. You know, the ones you've had sitting around for the last year and never got around to reading?

- Use stickers! You can basically buy a sticker for anything on Etsy these days. Just search Etsy for "weight loss sticker" or "travel stickers" or "write a book" stickers and you'll find something cute that you can use, with no creativity required! I just made those exact searches on Etsy and am officially $20 poorer, but you should see the cute stickers I just ordered!

Having a vision board makes your goals concrete and attainable. Once a goal has been defined, it becomes reachable.

In the next chapter, I'm going to share some specific styles of vision boards with you that I think will help you gain some focus, and, in turn, reach your goals faster.

Big-Picture Best Life Vision Boards

When you think of a vision board, you are probably thinking of a Big-Picture Vision Board. This type of vision board includes big, sweeping goals (earn a million dollars! go somewhere exotic! buy a big house!) and tends to be all-encompassing (and also, lose weight! spend time with the kids! read more books!). They might be big (like, an actual giant board hanging on a wall) and will include images and words to remind you of your Best Life.

This might even be something you do with your entire family.

These types of vision boards are helpful because they remind you of your Best Life. They feature your priorities. They're who you *are*, but have yet to become (mine includes donkeys in the backyard).

If this type of vision board is your jam, I encourage you to be specific. Like, super specific.

As you'll see when we talk about other types of vision boards, the more specific you can be, the better. It's easier to reach a goal you can clearly see.

But a quick note about being specific:

It's okay if you don't have a clear picture of exactly what you want, right this second. It's okay if you know you want to travel abroad, but don't have a particular spot in mind (Morocco, Norway, and Scotland, I'm coming for you!). Life is all about figuring out what we want, right?

A few years ago, Charles and I were driving to dinner. We didn't have the kids with us, which was very rare at the time (*date night!*). At the time, my blog was a baby. I knew it was taking me somewhere, but I didn't know where it was going. I mean, I really, really, really *knew* it was taking me somewhere. I could literally feel it in my gut, like a gentle tug saying, "Follow me! Do this!"

But I didn't know *where* it was taking me. Not yet.

I was trying to verbalize this to Charles as we cruised down the highway, headed to dinner. "I know it's the right thing, and there's something here—I just don't know what it looks like yet!" I explained.

Now, part of me was super afraid to even admit that I was on this path. I mean, who was I, anyway? I had quit my job at an insurance agency in Dallas (a job I liked) to be a stay-at-home mom. I wasn't tech-savvy (outside of some mad Excel skills). I didn't have a following on my blog. I didn't know what kind of blogger I wanted to be, or how I planned on making money doing this. In fact, no one even knew about my blog, because I was embarrassed to share myself in that way.

But I knew that I was basically going to make up a job for myself, because I liked to work, I'm creative, and when you work for yourself, you can wear leggings all day.

If I had made a vision board at that time, it might have vaguely said, in some form, that I wanted to be a full-time blogger, creator, or writer. But it would have been vague, y'all. I didn't know what my current job looked like at that time, and I was too timid to even call myself a blogger.

As I continued down this wide and debris-strewn path, it's gradually narrowed and today the road in front of me is startlingly clear (while still filled with the occasional surprise, some magical, and some *not so much*).

That same vision board, today, would show a much more clearly defined picture of my career path.

My advice is to *do the best you can*. Be as specific as you can. Be ready to update your vision board, or scrap it completely for a new one, when the time feels right.

With all that in mind, let's talk about the logistics of creating a Big-Picture Best Life Vision Board (you can totally skip this step and move on to something else if this doesn't resonate with you).

Here's an example of my current Big-Picture Best Life Vision Board. Most of it's pretty specific, because that's where I am at this point of my life. Yours may be different. If it makes you feel better, mine would have looked much, much different five years ago.

Like I mentioned earlier, you can use anything for your vision board—a page in your journal or planner would be perfect. But if you really want to spread out and include lots of your Best Life dreams in your board, use the ideas on page 60 for inspiration.

1. Create a rough draft. I've even given you room for it at the back of this book! (And if your rough draft is all you need, use this space and call it a day—you can always come back later and turn it into something fancy.)

2. Grab a stack of magazines and spend some time flipping through the pages and cutting out the pictures that resonate with you. See something that reminds you of the life you want to live? Cut it out!

3. Go online and find pictures of your Best Life. You want to ride an Arabian horse across the desert in Morocco? (I totally do.) Find the trip you want to take. Print out the itinerary. Stick it on your vision board. It's okay to dream big, y'all.

4. Download quotes that make you smile and touch your soul. Inspirational quotes are a dime a dozen, and while I'm a total sucker for some motivational words, I know they can get, well, cheesy. The key is to find words that make your energy buzz and your spirits lift (words have a powerful way of doing that). I have a few quotes that have stuck with me for years and that I hold near and dear to my heart. Keep important words front and center in your life. I've done some of the work for you—I've collected some fun, inspiring, not-cheesy quotes and made them cute for you—you can print these off and use them in your vision board.

Annual Vision Board

Last year, the kids and I watched *Fuller House* (season 2) on Netflix. It was December, and I was a day or two away from turning thirty-nine years old. In one episode, DJ, the oldest sister in the show's Tanner family, is also turning thirty-nine, and she pulls out the vision board she created when she turned thirty-eight, full of all the stuff she wanted to do before she turned thirty-nine.

Of course, it was silly and included things like, "sing with the Backstreet Boys" (not that I wouldn't be into that if I had the chance), but it totally got me thinking.

What did I want to accomplish in the next year?

When I turn forty, am I going to look back and think, "Wow, I wish I had done this, that, and the other?" Or will I look back at my awesome year and think, *"Hell yeah, I killed it this year!"* (I'm going with the latter).

So I did what anyone would do. *I took my inspiration where I could find it* (you truly never know when inspiration will strike!), and the very next day, I made an Annual Vision Board with all the things I wanted to do in the upcoming year.

Right now, as I write this book, I am eight months into my thirty-ninth year and I have already accomplished many of the things on my vision board.

You can see for yourself on page 66 (and you can also copy this format exactly—download this very vision board template by scanning the QR code here).

While your Big-Picture Best Life vision board might include a vacation to Norway (me! me! me!), your Annual Vision Board might include something like, "Save $5,000 for Vacation in Norway."

These types of actionable goals, with a time line attached, are very effective pieces of the puzzle when trying to scheme up ways to do crazy things like vacation in Norway.

Let me give you an example on a smaller, more personal level.

As I mentioned in the last chapter, I realized years ago that I was on a blogging journey and that it was taking me somewhere Super Cool. I didn't know exactly where that was, though.

Over the years, I have slowly and steadily working on my blog (I mean, *really* steadily, y'all . . . while at thirty-nine years old I'm still a horrible housekeeper who can't cook, I have applied myself to my career *like whoa* and I have been working on my blog zealously for years now). It's been slow. I was never that person who started making $10,000 a month six months after starting my blog, and I was never that blogger who won't stop popping up in your Facebook feed to teach you how she gets millions of pageviews each month after just starting her blog. No, it wasn't like that at all. It was slow and steady.

One thing I knew, from the beginning, was that I wanted to write a book.

But to want to write a book and to say out loud "I want to write a book" and mean it are two very different things.

When I wanted to get serious about my blogging, I hired a blogger that I admire (hi, Jill from BabyRabies.com!) for some consulting. She sent me a questionnaire to get a feel for where I was in my blogging journey, and one of the questions asked me to define a big, scary goal of mine that I had.

I was embarrassed to even write it, but I did. *I want to write a book,* I wrote. *I just don't know what that looks like right now.* (Or, that's basically the gist of what I wrote.)

Over the years, I'd mention to my husband that I wanted to write a book, but I still didn't know what it was. Then, at the beginning of this year (right after I turned thirty-nine), I told him that this was the year I was going to write my book. I went from having no clear book topic to suddenly having several, and my issue was no longer what I would write about, *but what would I write about first?*

I set that intention loud and clear. I said it out loud. I wrote it down. And before I knew it, I "magically" had an offer to write a book. I use the term "magical" loosely, because while the circumstances and the process around this book certainly do feel magical, it boils down to years of hard work and a set goal finally aligning, and there's nothing magic about hard work.

My Big-Picture Best Life vision board (which didn't exist at the time I started blogging) would have included "write a book" on it, but it would have been a teeny little blip on the board that I was almost too afraid to believe could be true.

But by the beginning of this year, "write a book" was a major goal that took center stage *for this year*. It was important for me to define that I would be writing a book this year—even if it wasn't published, I was still going to write it.

Use your Annual Vision Board to look at your upcoming year. Start it now, start it on January 1, start it on your birthday, start it on your favorite holiday . . . it doesn't matter when the year starts. It matters that you have a time line attached to it.

Use the inspiration on the following pages to craft an Annual Vision Board. Remember that this vision board will be full of goals you want to complete in the next 365 days—this is a great chance to take some of your Big-Picture Best Life goals and break them into doable mini goals.

1. Use any format you feel comfortable with. Again, a big board for your office will work—but something smaller that you can keep in your planner or on your desk might be more suitable.

2. Use numbers! This is a great time to quantify your goals. Your Big-Picture Vision Board might say you want to be debt-free. Your Annual Vision Board might say you want to pay off $10,000 in debt. Being specific with numbers makes your goal crystal clear.

3. Try using a list format. I broke my annual vision board out into categories (like Books I Will Read), and listed all the books I wanted to read this year. Not only is it super handy when I can't decide what to read, but it was also easy to make. Lists are easy.

4. Fill it with stickers. Sticker paper is cheap! I turned some of my favorite pictures from Facebook and Instagram into stickers and used them on my vision board.

5. Use the template on page 68 to create an Annual Vision Board (or, just sketch in some ideas for a rough draft).

words I will live by

make it HAPPEN

BE WHO i want to be

believe in yourself

Hustle

FOCUS

I AM DEBT FREE!

DO WHAT MAKES YOU HAPPY

Girl BOSS

She Believed She Could so she Did

THINGS I WILL DO

WORK OUT

PLACES I WILL GO Seattle California - air force museum

HOW I WILL FEEL

FOCUS

GOOD MORNING SUNSHINE

LIFE IS AN ADVENTURE

JOY

TRUST THE TIMING OF YOUR LIFE

PRIORITIES I WILL REMEMBER

volunteer horses

KIDS

BOOKS I WILL READ

Man in the High Castle · the Body Book · the Perfect Horse · The Hidden Life of Trees · The name of the Wind · Neverwhere · Orange is the New Black · Two Outlander Books · Find Your North Star · Cinder Series · The Power of Now · The Book of Life · Talking As Fast As I Can · The Lovely Bones · The Gifts of Imperfection · Everyone Brave is Forgiven · Being in Balance · Dangerous Women · The Eighty Dollar Champion

Write a Book (or 3)

ways I will love

KIDS

Books by kids

LITTLE THINGS

Patience + Love

Family TIME ♥

Think HAPPY Thoughts

my whole HEART

Having a hard time coming up with ideas? Here are some topics you might want to include in your Annual Vision Board:

- Pay off debt
- Save for vacation
- Buy a new home
- Lose weight
- Book list
- Start a blog
- Start a new business
- Get up earlier
- Keep the house clean
- Get a raise
- Quit smoking
- Make a healthy lifestyle change
- Get a dog (or a donkey!)
- Start taking music lessons
- Learn a new language
- Travel somewhere amazing (be specific!)

List your own ideas below:

WORDS I WILL LIVE BY

THINGS I WILL DO

BOOKS I WILL READ

PLACES I WILL GO

HOW I WILL FEEL

PRIORITIES I WILL REMEMBER

WAYS I WILL LOVE

If you want to make it *super* simple, download this Annual Vision Board template and just fill it in.

Specific Vision Boards

When I was twenty-eight, my career path veered unexpectedly into the corporate world. Previously, my jobs had involved animals, kids, or a combination of both.

Working in a real office (with coworkers! And cubicles! And a deli in the building!), wearing business casual, and slogging through rush-hour traffic twice a day was my new world.

And you know what?

I was terrified.

Like, *legit*. When I got home from the office after my first day of work, I burst into tears. The day had been a monumental stress fest that reminded me over and over again that I had no business being there. I didn't know how to open Excel, let alone create a spreadsheet! I had never used Outlook for email before. I was nervous, and shy, and *I couldn't even work the fax machine*.

I literally had no idea what PPO even stood for, and here I was working at an insurance agency.

Despite all this, my boss (who was *so* awesome) had hired me. She'd believed in me. She thought I could do it. And so did Charles (who was also super pragmatic about the whole thing and said, "Look, they spent a bunch of money finding you and hiring you, they're not going to fire you the first week").

Slowly, *so slowly*, my confidence grew.

As I waded through all the insurance acronyms, I did my very best to keep up with the coworker who was training me. One day, after I had been there for months (still not fired!), I started asking some detailed questions about HSAs (totally not going to start on health insurance here, I promise).

"I know you've already told me this a million times," I said to the ever-patient and oh-so-kind coworker of mine. "But now I'm ready to learn it."

And I was. I had absorbed all I could about the big picture health insurance topics, and I was ready to dig deeper.

And that's how our goals often work too, isn't it? It takes us a while to really know what we want—or what we need to know. You might know you want a bigger house (or room for some donkeys out back). Or maybe you know you want to have more energy. Or perhaps take a trip to Europe. But that's vague. That's an idea, a feeling, a hunch of what's actually to come.

> It takes us a while to really know what we want—or what we need to know.

At some point, you'll be ready to clarify those goals and start acting on them. You'll know you want a bigger house that is brick, in a particular neighborhood, and that has three bathrooms. You'll know that you need to exercise, and that yoga is the way to go. You'll decide that it's going to be Europe indeed, but specifically Spain.

You're ready to dig deeper and zero in on more specific concepts and visions of your goal.

You already have the tools to create a beautiful Big-Picture Best Life Vision Board and a more specific Annual Vision Board.

So let's break it down even more.

There are a lot of reasons why you might do this. In some cases, you might have individual goals that are Very Important to you. Those deserve their own space where you can direct your intention, love, and game plan.

Or maybe you have some little goals that really don't necessitate an entire vision board and the work it entails, but you still want to keep them front and center.

Super-Specific Vision Boards are perfect for this.

A Super-Specific Vision Board might look like any of these:

- Monthly goals

- Single goal (if you want to pay off $10,000 in debt this year, you might break it up into smaller goals of $1,000 each)

- Lists (books you want to read, movies you want to see, rooms in your house you need to deep-clean)

- Your to-do list (that's right . . . your to-do list might seem mundane, but I bet completing it sure makes you feel good!)

Now, let me say this:

Don't get so excited about creating vision boards that you spend all your time imagining your goals and creating beautiful vision boards, and no time actually working on them. And also? Don't think for one second that you have to create a fancy vision board for every little goal.

This should never be a chore! It should be fun, inspire you, and help you connect with your goals in a fresh and personal way.

It can be overwhelming if you think you have to create something beautiful every time you have a goal you want to accomplish. For many people, simply writing it down is enough. For others, just thinking about your goal and keeping your eyes on the prize is enough. But for others, it can be extremely helpful to create at least some type of vision-board-esque reminder of, well, *our visions*.

I feel like I'm always writing down goals. Writing down goals is fine. Writing down goals is fun! But I like to give some goals—usually those with time lines or a big payoff attached—a little extra love.

It's okay to keep it simple. It's okay to put some stickers on an index card and carry it around in your purse. It's okay to decorate your calendar with some doodles of goals you want to meet that month. It's okay to fill a Word doc with important goals in pretty fonts and call it a day (ooooh, get some bubble fonts, and then you can color them!).

Art Journaling and Vision Boards

When I was in tenth grade, my English teacher taught us how to take notes. Now, in theory, we already knew how to take notes. This was an honors English class, and many of us had been in honors classes since seventh grade. We knew a thing or two about taking notes (if by taking notes, you mean structuring the teacher's lesson into an outline of sorts on your paper that you take home and try to memorize).

But Mrs. Jones taught us a completely different system for note taking and it literally changed my life. It was exactly how I *wanted* to take notes, but it was like I needed permission to let myself work in this fashion (I'm a rule follower).

I don't have the scientific study to back it up, but she told us that if you took notes in a nonlinear fashion and used doodles, shapes, and colors, you'd be more likely to actually remember the content of your notes.

She encouraged us to write outside the lines, fill in the margins, and add drawings, arrows, boxes, big, bold letters, and color to our notes. Basically, I felt like I was doodling and writing notes to my friend for the entire forty-five-minute period I was in her class every day, *and it was heaven.*

What I discovered was that this totally worked. When we read *The Great Gatsby* and discussed the symbolism of the colors F. Scott Fitzgerald used (green! white! gold!), I drew pictures of everything. I wrote "gold" in big fancy letters and surrounded it with dollar signs.

When it came time to take the test, I knew exactly what each color stood for. I could see the drawings in my head as I took the test.

An art journal can be used for anything from a to-do list to a goal tracker to an actual journal and literally anything in between.

I have applied this method to all of my note taking since (it's how I memorized the periodic table in eleventh grade—unfortunately, I can only remember a few of the elements today).

I love applying these techniques to my own "life notes"—goals, things I need to remember or do, even my to-do list.

This is why I love art journaling.

If you've never art journaled before, let me give you a quick rundown of Art Journaling 101.

Any journal will work (lined, blank, graph paper), but I prefer one filled with dotted grid paper. You use it to create whatever notes you want to create. To keep it organized, many people will use the first page or two as a table of contents (you could also use the pages at the end as an index).

The owner of the journal numbers the pages (usually) and fills in the table of contents as they go. An art journal can be used for anything from a to-do list to a goal tracker to an actual journal and literally anything in between.

It can be gorgeous and elaborate, or it can be simple text. Don't be intimidated by the beautiful journals created by artists that keep popping up on Instagram. Yours doesn't need to be that fancy (but I bet you'll find that the more you work in your journal, the more artistic and creative you'll become).

Check out the art journaling samples on the next couple of pages.

Here's what I love about journaling in general: you can fill your journal with tons of different types of content, and have it all in one place.

This is the perfect place for visualizing your goals (especially if you want to keep your vision boards portable, small, and all in one place)! You can include multiple boards in your journal.

BOOKS I WANT TO READ:

hustle

gratitude is everything

Yoga Classes

With Love · With Love · With Love · With Love

movies i want to see

☐ the mountains between us
☐ home again

PASS ME THE POPCORN

POP CORN

movie night!
at home

5

It's also highly functional, and a perfect place for creating your plan of attack, tracking your progress, and keeping your day-to-day notes in one place.

Because art journaling is so fun, and such a great tool, I've included several pages in this book for you to use. If you feel stuck, here are some ideas to get the creative juices flowing:

- Vision board (Best Life, annual goals, monthly goals, etc.)
- Habit tracker
- Priorities (Make a page for your priorities so you'll always have them in front of you. You can use pictures of the people you love, your pets, your dream house: anything that reminds you why you do what you do and makes you feel centered.)
- Cut the fat (Dedicate a portion to the time-wasters in your life. Writing them down and referring to them will help you remember *what you don't need to be wasting your time on*.)
- Things that make you happy (Seriously! Fill a whole page or ten with the things you love.)
- Schedules
- To-do lists
- Places you want to go
- Books you want to read
- Homework assignments
- Cleaning tasks
- Journaling

Let Your Creative Self Shine with Pretty Vision Boards

When I decided to start meal planning (like, really meal planning, not just trying to figure out dinner plans at the last minute while two small children cried at my feet), I knew that all I really needed was a piece of paper and a pencil. That was it. No fancy meal-planning tools required.

But I also believe, firmly, that some things are just more fun when they're pretty. And I had this idea for a particular product that would be way more functional that just a piece of paper, so I set about trying to find one. When I couldn't, I made my own.

This is how I ended up making a pretty meal planner that turned into a fun little side project that turned into a full-time business for myself and Charles. All because I wanted something functional *and* fun to look at.

You may not care about pretty, and I am here to tell you that is 100 percent A-OK. My mother-in-law is the single most organized person I know, and she manages with a pocket calendar and a pencil (well, she *managed* with a pocket calendar and a pencil; I've upgraded her to a fancy planner).

Things don't have to be pretty to be effective. It's important that you understand this, because I don't want you to get frustrated when your finished product doesn't look exactly like you imagined it would (okay, maybe, very possibly, I am talking to myself and the perfectionist that hides deep inside me).

But for the sake of this chapter, let's talk about making things pretty (even if you have *no* artsy or crafty skills).

I'm going to talk about vision board supplies and share with you some of my favorite tools for making things fancy (even though I am not fancy at all in real life).

Let's Talk Materials

Here's something cool about vision boards: they can be whatever you want them to be. That means they can look however you want them to look.

Here are some suggestions for different materials that you might employ to create your masterpiece(s):

- Poster board—Poster boards are the super thick and sturdy boards you can find in the craft section at your local Walmart or Target. These are great for a vision board you want to prominently feature on display, because they hold up really well.

- Card stock—I should buy stock in card stock. I use it all the time. My favorite is the store brand they sell at Michaels (this version is really cheap, too). You can cut it to any size you need. The paper will hold up well if you have it in a notebook or a folder and plan on touching it regularly.

- Magazines—This is the perfect way to use up all the magazines you have sitting around the house. Spend some time ripping out your favorite pages or cutting out pictures. Don't just cut out the stuff you want in your own life. Also cut out the ads, color schemes, and fonts you find appealing.

- Internet—If you don't have magazines on hand (or can't find a friend who wants to unload some), have no fear—the Internet has you covered! Search the Internet for pictures of what you love, stories that inspire you, and websites that make you feel motivated.

- Your phone—If you're thinking about priorities and things that are important to you, you probably have a wealth of pictures of those exact things on your phone. Print off your favorite pictures of your kids, your home, your pets, whatever. Making your vision boards feel personal will make them even more relevant.

- Scissors—If you're going to be cutting stuff out and then staring at it all year long, invest in a nice pair of scissors. Trust me.

- Pencil—You can go willy-nilly and just start gluing stuff all over your board. But you might want to sketch out where you want to glue things, or pencil in your handwriting before finalizing it with a Sharpie.

- Sticky stuff—Glue will work, but I prefer adhesive rollers you can buy at any craft store. These are incredibly easy to use and there's no drying time. Also, you can use them on small spaces. If you go with glue, pick a sticky one (glue sticks aren't always sticky enough to hold everything).

- Creative media—Basically, whatever else you can think of. Paints. Markers. Cotton balls (those would make some fun clouds or snow, right?). Brochures from a destination you want to visit. Pressed flowers. A dollar bill, to symbolize the 999,999 others ones you're going to earn that year (hey, that's a good idea, actually—totally going to do that on my own). Think outside the box, because that is exactly what you're going to be doing as you work on reaching these goals.

The key here is to remember that you can literally make your vision board anything you want it to be. Let it be reflective of you. Have fun with it!

Give Yourself Positive Labels and Affirmations (Without Feeling Cheesy)

I used to feel like saying affirmations every day was cheesy. To be totally honest, I thought it was kind of *woowoo*, you know what I mean? I guess I didn't believe they could make a difference, and the whole concept of talking about how awesome I was, or how much money I had (when I wasn't necessarily feeling awesome, and didn't have any money) just felt *weird*.

But that's not how I feel anymore. Over the years, I've learned to embrace affirmations and take them very seriously.

Here's why.

Words matter.

There's a reason we are all familiar with the quote, "The pen is mightier than the sword." It's because *we all understand the power of words*.

But still, it can feel awkward at first. When I first started my affirmation practice, it felt foreign, a little uncomfortable, and even a little weird.

Go ahead. Call me a weirdo! I'm here to tell you that what we tell ourselves—and *what we call ourselves*—matters.

Every night, before I fall asleep, I run through a list of affirmations that ring true with me. They remind me that I am well, I am kind, I am creative. I have others that are super specific to a particular project I might be working on, or a way I might be feeling. They remind me that I get to be in control of how I feel, how I act, and what I bring into my life.

And speaking of what I bring into my life.

One night, I realized that I didn't have enough positive self-talk or affirmations or what-you-want-to-call-it to cover all the things I needed at that moment. Mostly, a large influx of cash.

So as I lay in bed that night, I heard myself say (in my head—you don't have to say daily affirmations out loud if you don't want to), "I have everything that I want. I have everything that I need."

You guys. I had this weird, warm flash of what I can only explain as *knowing* through my entire body. In a heartbeat, I realized that I actually already had everything that I ever needed and everything that I ever wanted.

It sounds cheesy, but it was so profound. Almost like a warm hand from another universe was gently laid upon me and gave me startling clarity for just a skip in time.

Of course, once I realized I already have everything I want or need, I quickly amended it to something more specific, like, "I have $250,000 in my bank account." (No warm Hand of the Universe came forth to tell me I already have that!)

I'm making light of a serious subject, but I'm also serious as a heart attack at the same time.

Kind of like that affirmation.

I *do* have everything I want. I have my family, and I have my health.

I *do* have everything I need. I have food, air, clean water, and a warm place to sleep at night.

It sounds weird, I know—but realizing that I already have everything I need made it seem like filling in all the little details should be easy. After all, they're just that—little details, when compared to the things that really matter. I want $250,000 in my bank account? Well—make it happen. I want a house with donkeys in my backyard? Well—what's stopping me?

Your turn! Give yourself some positive labels and write them down on the next page. If you feel stuck, here are some you can use:

- Kind
- Compassionate
- Strong
- Healthy
- Fit
- Capable
- Brave
- Social
- Friendly
- Rich (don't judge yourself for wanting some extra g's!)

While you're at it, create some affirmations for yourself. Say them at night, or when you meditate, or when you wake up. Email them to yourself. Stick them on your mirror. Or just keep them in here. Here are some examples if you're getting stuck:

- I am healthy and strong.
- I am starting a new business.
- I am getting a raise.
- My bank account has $250,000 (or go big, and let's say a million) in it.
- My donkeys live in my backyard.

Part III

Implement Planning Strategies

You Are a Creative

When I was a kid, I spent a lot of time at my grandparents' home, a little white brick house a half mile from the beach. One day, my brother and I were visiting while my parents went to watch a golf tournament (such a strange memory, as I don't recall my dad ever golfing or my mom caring for it either, but, there they were).

My brother and I played in "the back room," a space with hardy utility carpet in a funky gold color with an orange and avocado green print, and wood paneling covering a wall full of cabinets. In this room, for as long as I could remember, was a big flat basket full of broken crayons and dull stubs of old pencils.

We really wanted to watch the golf tournament to see if we might spot my parents on TV, but my grandmother was engaged in *The Price Is Right*.

So we did what any kid would do. We decided to build our own TV so we could watch the tournament.

Armed with a couple of boxes, the basket of crayons, and some rubber bands we snagged from the impressive collection my grandfather kept in an old coffee can next to the water heater, we set to work making our own television.

It never occurred to me, not for one second, that we couldn't make an actual television with boxes, crayons, and a handful of rubber bands.

Unfortunately, our idea did not pan out and our creation instead became a box guitar, which you totally *could* make with a shoebox and rubber bands.

> My creative might not look like someone else's creative, but that's okay.

I see the same confidence in my daughter. At six years old, she doesn't think for one second that she's not creative.

A few weeks ago, I found her in my office, digging through my craft supplies, with a box of markers under her arm.

"Can I have that oatmeal container?" she asked, referencing an empty canister I was holding on to for a craft idea I had yet to get around to actually making (typical).

I weighed the pros and cons. Con: I would have to eat another cylinder's worth of oatmeal before I had another container for my craft. Pro: If I gave the container away, I could just forget about the craft.

"Sure, you can have it," I said. "What are you going to do with it?"

She looked at me in an exasperated sort of way that I imagine daughters have been looking at mothers for all of eternity and said, "I don't know yet, but you *know* how creative I am, Mom."

Like, *duh*, Mom.

Oh, to have that that unshakeable confidence in our own ability to make something!

I want to keep that alive in me. My creative might not look like someone else's creative, but that's okay. I'm still creative.

And so are you.

Your creative may not look like my creative. It might not look like the "creative" we think of when scroll through Instagram. It might not look like anything you've ever stumbled across on Pinterest.

That is totally okay.

When I worked in the corporate world, my boss was always encouraging us to be creative and think outside the box. She would tell us that she wasn't creative, and that she was better with things like numbers and spreadsheets.

But I learned a valuable lesson working for her.

Creativity comes in all shapes, sizes, and forms.

She was creative. In fact, she was the one I went to when I had been staring at a spreadsheet all day and couldn't find the answer I was looking for. She was the one who helped clients really put together benefits packages that worked for all of their employees. She was *totally* creative!

You are the same way.

Maybe you're an artist. Maybe you're a whiz with numbers and can come up with ten different ways to solve the same problem. Maybe you're the master at packing with a Tetris-like efficiency.

I have a friend named Jesika who is the most creative person I know. Most likely, she is the most creative person you would ever know if you met her, too. She's *that* creative. When I am around her and see her work, I feel like maybe I'm not that good at what I do. I mean, she's a real artist, you guys.

One night, I was out to dinner with her and my other BFF, Sara. The three of us were doodling on kid menus as we waited for our dinner to arrive (and no, we did not have any kids with us). I was coloring expertly within the lines, and my menu was looking super cute. But Jesika? She had elaborated on the rather boring menu characters and created an entire world.

Sara, meanwhile, was not really interested in drawing at all.

"You guys suck!" she said (you can say things like that to your best friend, or at least my friends and I can). "I see Jesika's drawing and I don't even want to try!"

I totally got it. I felt the same way. My piddle-y little capability to stay in the lines was nothing compared to Jesika's fine art.

I still have feelings like that today, even with a blog and a business that both started because I like to make things.

It's easy to feel like I'm not creative enough. Like others are better at the things I am trying to do. But what I've learned is that it's okay, and normal, to have those feelings. The important thing is, *how do I respond to those feelings?*

These days, I try not to play the comparison game.

I am creative. I am enough. And the creativity of others is beautiful and inspiring.

I love this quote from artist Mary Lou Cook:

"Creativity is inventing, experimenting, growing, taking risks, breaking rules, making mistakes, and having fun."—Mary Lou Cook

Creativity isn't just about making something cute. It's about creating new things, challenging yourself, failing, trying again . . . and enjoying the process as much as you can.

Let's talk about how creative *you* are, and how to get even more creative.

First, write this out below: *I am creative.*

_____

Now, we're going to try an exercise that I learned at a blogging conference. The conference was sponsored by Disney (and Disney is probably the definition of "creative," if you were to look it up), so you know this is the real deal. They told us that when they get a creative team together to brainstorm ideas, they dig deep. The first few ideas are just to help you scratch the surface. The next few ideas will get the juices flowing. But it's not until you get to fifteen or twenty ideas that things really start to take shape—this is when the creativity starts going to another level. The ideas are fresher and newer, and this is where it gets intense (in a good way). I have found the same to be true for myself.

Let's try it, shall we?

Think of a goal you have. On the next page, brainstorm ways to make that goal happen. Literally no idea is too crazy for this exercise. In fact, the crazier the better, because even if your idea feels very fringe lunatic-y, it's totally okay. There's probably some truth to it, and that will inspire even more ideas. So, go crazy. Write down all the ideas. Don't stop until you have at least twenty (but thirty is even better, and it's okay to be an overachiever here!).

How to Get Started Turning Those Dreams into Realities

"Do not give up. The beginning is always hardest."—unknown

It was 1991, and I was in my eighth grade English class. With my permed bangs (I still can't figure out what I was thinking when I told the hair lady, "Perm my bangs! But *only* my bangs"), my three-ring binder full of lined, pink paper and covered in doodles of horses, and my best friend seated next to me, I was more concerned about passing notes than immersing myself in my education.

One particular day, a fellow student started complaining about the writing prompt our teacher had given us.

"I don't know what to write!" he whined.

"Just start," she said. "Just write *something*."

"But I can't think of *anything* to write about for this prompt!" he protested.

"Then make something up," she said. "Make something up, and just start writing."

She wasn't telling us to become liars. She was teaching us to *be creative*.

She was telling us to *just start* doing something, and the rest would follow.

And she was right.

I walked away with some very valuable lessons that year. I didn't realize it at the time, but the words of my eighth grade English teacher, Mrs. Cavanaugh, have stuck with me for life and created a springboard for many of the projects and ideas I've seen come to fruition.

> It doesn't matter where you start, so long as you do.

Whenever I find that I'm stuck on something—be it cleaning the house, writing a blog post, or making healthy choices—I find myself saying, "Just start. Just start somewhere."

And the rest? Well, *the rest follows.*

Life is a work in progress. But we can shape it. We can listen to our creative selves and cultivate the "doer" inside all of us and Make Things Happen.

If I had a dollar for every time someone (including me!) said, "I just don't know where to start!" I'd be a rich lady. Well, except for all the dollars I'd have to pay myself. Because I've said it as many times as the next person. In fact, I still find myself saying those seven words when a new project idea pops up.

I just don't know where to start.

The hardest part is always starting. I believe this, wholeheartedly! Ideas are easy. Everybody has them! If you think you don't have great ideas, you're wrong—you just need to learn how to tap into them (and we're going to talk about that).

But how do you get from *an idea* to completing your manuscript, decorating your house, or taking that dream vacation?

Unfortunately, these things don't (most of the time!) just happen. These things all require work. They require energy and creativity and ideas and *implementation and follow-through.*

Here's what I've learned, and here's my advice to you—it doesn't matter where you start, so long as you do.

Just start somewhere.

In theory, we would all start at the beginning of our projects and diligently chip away at them, step-by-step, until we've completed our masterpiece or reached our goal. The reality is a lot different for most of us, though. For example, the first thing I wrote in this book was the story in this chapter about my eighth grade English teacher (and my permed bangs). I thought that was the beginning of this book, but it turns out it wasn't.

It was important to me that I just start writing something, and that's the story that materialized. Timely, at that—a story about just getting started popped up when I literally needed to just get started, already.

I hear this a lot of time in my real life, with people who want to start blogs. It's so overwhelming, they just don't know where to begin.

I've been there. I totally get it. If you're not technical (I am so not technical), the very idea of starting your own website can be crippling. Since a lot of people actually do ask me this question, I'll give you the quick rundown of how I started my blog.

I started my blog on a free blogging platform (Blogger) in 2006. From 2006 to 2011, I blogged occasionally, when the mood hit me. When I decided to get serious about it, I was so overwhelmed with all the information out there that I almost never started.

Instead, though, I decided to do what I could with what I had. I had a free blogging platform. I had limited time and a baby that never wanted to be put down. I had literally zero photography skills.

I would write, a couple of paragraphs here and there, while nursing the baby (God bless you, nursing pillow and laptop), or while I stood at the counter and bounced from foot to foot as Claire fell asleep in the baby carrier. It was slow going, y'all.

One day at a time. Some days, one sentence at a time.

I didn't have any crazy expectations for making money or gaining lots of readers right away. It was just important to me to do the work.

Slowly, I started learning about the business of blogging. I hired someone to redesign my site (still on Blogger). I went to a blogging conference. I joined some blogging forums online. I found my blogging tribe (hi, tribe!).

Most importantly, I put in the work.

It didn't matter that I didn't have a beautiful site or social media accounts. It didn't even matter that I didn't have blog readers. It only mattered that I was doing something, and that I was building on what I did know.

And that is my number one piece of advice to everyone—just start, and keep on keepin' on. Eventually, you'll get there—or at least, you'll get to the next level, which in turn will lead you one step closer to your goal.

A lot of people don't want to hear that, though. They want the quick and easy way to reach their goals, and I'm afraid I can't be of much help in that situation.

My successes are all wrapped up in determination and hard work. You've got to put in the work!

And that is what I hope for you, too. I hope you will identify what you want. And then I hope you'll put plans in place to achieve those very things.

You can do it, and I believe in you!

Action Plan

Fall is a very busy time of year for my planner business. This is when we launch new products and gear up for holiday shopping. *It can be very, very stressful.*

You see, I'm a procrastinator by nature (as I write this, I am frighteningly close to the submission deadline for this book). When I first heard the quote, "If you wait until the last minute to do something, it only takes a minute to do it," I was like *yesssssss*. Finally, someone *gets* me!

When I was a senior in high school, we had to complete a huge "real life" project that was required to graduate. It involved filling out a job application, creating a résumé, and putting together a presentation that included a ten-minute speech about what we wanted to do with our lives when we graduated from high school.

We learned about this project during the first week of school.

I had literally nine months to complete it.

So when did I start? *Around 11 p.m. the night before I was scheduled to give my presentation at 7:30 the next morning.*

7:30! It was the first time slot of the day, and I'm sure I chose it because that would mean I had the rest of the day off. It certainly wasn't because I'm a morning person. (It definitely wasn't because of that. If you ever get the chance, ask my husband how much I love mornings. Ha!)

Around 10 p.m. or so, I thought, I should really go buy my supplies to make this presentation.

I had already decided I'd talk about how I planned to work with horses (which I totally ended up doing!). So I figured the rest would be easy. Glue some horse pictures to a piece of tagboard, write up some talking points, fill out the job application, and call it a night.

Ha! Hahahahaha*hahahaha*.

I drove to the nearest drugstore and bought some markers, glue, and a few pieces of white tagboard for the presentation.

Then I sat down, with all of my crap spread out before me across our living room floor, and got to work.

I should add here that my mom, a fellow Wait Till the Last Minute Night Owl, was still awake, working in the kitchen until around midnight. She understood!

The first thing I did was pull out the instructions. And guess what?

This was way more work than I had anticipated. The requirements were in-depth, and I had to turn in a typed version of my talk (which totally threw a kink in my plans, because I was going to wing it). Oh, and did I mention a passing grade was required to graduate?

I sighed, resigned to the work ahead, and started clipping horse pictures out of my magazines.

Somewhere around 3 a.m., hours before I had to wake up and wear "something I would wear to a job interview," I wrapped up the project and went to bed.

Three hours later, I woke up and dug through my closet (why hadn't I found a suitable outfit the night before, I wondered). I wore what any self-respecting eighteen-year-old would have worn to job interview in 1996. A pink short-sleeved turtleneck, a miniskirt, black thigh highs, and my knock-off Doc Martens.

2018 me is cringing just thinking about it. But 1996 me was totally into it!

So anyway, I showed up on time, aced the presentation (thanks, Public Speaking 4-H project!), and walked away spent, promising myself that I would *never* wait until the last minute on another project for as long as I lived. Which is hilarious, because as I write this, my son is sitting at the kitchen table, forty-five minutes past his bedtime, working on an assignment that's due tomorrow.

All that to say, I procrastinate just as well as the next person.

But I've stopped letting procrastination rule my life (well, except for the part where I'm up against a close deadline with this book and my son is up past his bedtime working on tomorrow's homework). It's okay to be last minute, but it's not okay to be unprepared. A plan of attack is everything, and if you know what you're going to do, and how you're going to do it, and how long it's going to take you, you will be able to get it done.

Earlier today, I was at the office with my husband, Charles. Fall is a really busy and stressful season, and we are always running behind on things. Right now, we have a bunch of projects we're trying to wrap up and they all have many moving pieces (I'm sure you can relate!).

Things are starting to feel extra chaotic and a little out of control. But I'm trying to write a book. And I have a deadline. And I've got a blog to run. And I'm trying to wrap up these product designs. *And the last thing I want to do is take two hours out of my day to make a production chart.*

But that's exactly what we did. We wrote down all the projects we are working on and came up with a chart to track the progress of each project, so we know exactly where are in the process.

It was a pain to sit down and do this. I wanted to stay home and write. Charles had things he needed to do, too. But when it was done, I felt in control of our situation, empowered, and even free. All of a sudden, I didn't feel like we were running from one thing to the next and back to the other thing and then over to that thing and then back to that second thing again. I knew exactly what was going on, and could start executing.

When you're busy, it can feel impossible to find the time to sit down and get organized (I hear this all the time when I talk to people about meal planning and they tell me, "I just don't have the time!"). I know how it is to feel like you're on a locomotive headed at a hundred miles an hour toward a

A plan of attack will help you reach your goals.

broken track. But I've also learned that you're better off taking a step back and trying to find the train's brakes than you are holding on and hoping for the best, you know what I mean?

While it can feel painful to set aside a couple hours, or even twenty minutes, to get organized, I promise you it's worth it.

A plan of attack will help you reach your goals. It will help you live your best life. It will help you manage the mundane day-to-day tasks that sidetrack us or often end up undone because *who has the time*, right?

I'm going to walk you exactly through how I plan for my days and my goals, and how I incorporate my vision boards to keep my eyes on the prize.

Your Goal Is Clear. Now You Need a Plan of Attack.

I love yoga! I'm not great at it, but for years now, yoga has been my default exercise. What's cool about yoga is that anyone can do it, at any level. A good yoga teacher will be able to teach the same poses to students at different levels at the same time, which means there is lots of room to grow.

Yoga can also be very spiritual and an amazing way to freshen and strengthen your mind—this is my formal yoga endorsement!

I took my first yoga class around fifteen years ago, and have fallen in and out of practice over the years. When I was young, and in amazing shape, there weren't many poses the instructor could throw at me that I couldn't handle, or wouldn't at least attempt.

But when I returned to yoga after having my second child, things had changed. For one thing, I was immensely tired five minutes into the class.

You guys. *We were still just sitting on the ground in a cross-legged position.*

With no core muscles to speak of, sitting up straight for five full minutes took an incredible amount of my strength. I can still remember the way my back strained as I struggled to keep my back tall, my shoulders relaxed, my jaw soft.

Months later, the teacher walked around the class as we all stood in triangle pose. Triangle pose, for the uninitiated, is a pose where your hips face forward, your legs spread with feet perpendicular to each other. You scoot your hips to one side and reach your upper body the other way. Then, you stretch your forward hand to the ground and your rear hand rises into the air. Your shoulders are stacked, and yoga teachers will tell you

> Your goal is your heart's way of pointing you in the right direction and telling you what you need to do to be happy!

to pretend your body is pressed between two panes of glass.

My fingertips grazed the ground. My strength was returning, and I was gaining some flexibility, but this pose was still hard.

Then the teacher said something profound (as yoga teachers often do). "Try to place your palm on the floor," she said. "You never know what can do until you try, and you might surprise yourself."

Because I'm a good student if nothing else, I decided to go for it, just like I had every other time she'd made this suggestion (without luck, I might add—those hamstrings wouldn't budge). I placed my palm on the ground.

I placed my palm on the ground.

Without being aware, I had given myself the flexibility and strength to take this pose to a new level. One day I couldn't do it, and the next day I could.

I opened into the stretch in an entirely new way. My mind sparkled with the revelation that *yesterday I wasn't able to do this, but today I am.*

All of the yoga classes building up to that one had given me the tools I needed to place my palm flat on the floor.

It seems like a silly thing, but it remains a great life lesson for me. Not only because it reminds me that I need yoga in my life to build strength, flexibility, and confidence in what my body is capable of, but also because it carried over into my non-yoga life (which is to say, the remaining 166 hours of the 168 hours in a week).

If you work hard and are consistent, one day you'll find yourself doing something you couldn't do before.

When you have a big huge goal you want to reach, it can be very intimidating. It can feel impossible, even. But since you have this goal in the first place, I believe that not only is it possible, it's also not that far out of reach. I believe that your goal is your heart's way of pointing you in the right direction and telling you what you need to do to be happy!

But if your goal is to make a million dollars and be debt-free, but you are behind on your rent, it can *feel* impossible. Or if your goal is to do a headstand, but you can't sit upright for five minutes without your back and stomach muscles cramping, you might be easily deterred.

By the way, making a million dollars and doing a yoga headstand are both goals of mine . . . I'll keep you posted!

I want to give you a Goal Plan system I use to break down my goals into actionable steps I can follow to reach my goals. It will work for you, too!

You can apply this Goal Plan system to any goal you are trying to reach, and any life you want to live.

Set Your Goal—Be very, very clear. Your goal is not "pay off some debt," it's "pay off $3,000 in debt" (or whatever number you choose). Write this down somewhere.

Set a Due Date—You'll work back from this due date.

Create Measurable Action Items—It's not enough to lay out simple groundwork, like "pay off extra each month." Take a look at your due date and determine how long you have to reach your goal. Then, put steps into place based on your time line. For example, if you've given yourself three months to pay off $3,000, we know that's $1,000 a month or $250/week. Your action item might be, "Pay off $250 a week."

You can also set goals, like, "Have a garage sale," or "sell old furniture on Facebook," to help you find the extra money you need to reach your main goal. You might include things like, "cash in change jar," or "apply grocery savings to debt."

Detail all of these steps in your Goal Plan.

Implement Your Action Plan—Apply yourself with tenacity to your goal. It's so easy to get sidetracked, distracted, or just give up. Find a supportive friend, an online group, or a family member to keep you accountable.

Track Your Progress—It might not seem like much when you pay off $250 out of $3,000. But after you've paid $250 a few times, you'll see it starting to add up. Be sure to track your progress as you work on your goal.

I made a little chart when I started writing this book, and each time I wrote one thousand words I checked off a box. It gave me a visual of how much I was accomplishing, and it helped me see how much I still had to work on so I could adjust my day as necessary. Finding a visual way to track your progress is so motivating!

Check In—Even if you aren't tracking your goal's progress (maybe your goal was to decorate your master bedroom, and it's an "all in one day" kind of thing), check in with it periodically. If you're decorating your bedroom, you're probably collecting paint colors or *making a vision board* or shopping for new furniture—be sure to set at least one or two "check-in" dates so you can sit down and see where you're at, and make adjustments as necessary.

Achieve Your Goal—Woohoo! This is the best part. Celebrate (I prefer donuts). If this goal is part of a bigger goal, take a day or two to celebrate your success and then the start the process all over again.

Need help organizing your Goal Plan? Use the goal trackers like the one shown here. Download your own goal plan pages by using the QR code.

DREAM BIG
goal trackers

Goal	Goal	Goal	Goal
RUN a 5K	decorate Master bedroom		
ACTION ITEMS	**ACTION ITEMS**	**ACTION ITEMS**	**ACTION ITEMS**
- Couch to 5K app on phone - new running shoes - armband - train 3x week	- pick color scheme - ideas on vision board - list out what I need to DIY - budget? - create master bedroom idea notebook		
NOTES	**NOTES**	**NOTES**	**NOTES**
→ need to start November 12th to reach goal by January 12th.	→ don't shop until vision board is done		
DUE DATE	**DUE DATE**	**DUE DATE**	**DUE DATE**
January 12	December 16		
Accomplished ☐	Accomplished ☐	Accomplished ☐	Accomplished ☐

Setting Your Intention

Maybe you're already familiar with the analogy I'm going to share below, made famous by Stephen Covey in *7 Habits of Highly Effective People*, but it's so important, I want to take a moment to discuss. If this is the first time you've heard of Stephen Covey, let me take a second and wholeheartedly recommend you read this book. Written in the eighties, it's still entirely relevant and always will be. I plan on reading everything Stephen Covey has written.

But back to this analogy.

A person has a stack of big rocks, a cup of sand, and a cup of pebbles that they need to combine into one vase. I don't know why, but I'm sure they have a very good reason.

They pour in the sand, then the pebbles, and finally dump in the big rocks. Of course, the sand and pebbles have taken up all the room in the vase because the vase isn't that big, and the big rocks don't all fit. Half of the big rocks are left outside of the vase, because there just isn't room for them.

Because this seems irrelevant, let's name the items.

Vase = your time.

Big Rocks = important things in your life that you must do. These are *the most important things* in your life (your priorities), and if you choose not to do these things, you can face serious consequences. For example, your health, your happiness, and perhaps your family and/or job could be affected if you can't get these big rocks to fit in your vase.

Pebbles = Things you have to do, but you can manage if something gets missed. Like picking up the house, or returning your library books on time.

Sand = Fillers. Social media, namely, but you can include

any time-waster here. But I'm going to say things like Facebook and Instagram, checking your emails constantly, binge-watching your favorite show when you have a bunch of other stuff you *should* be doing (big rocks!).

When we keep our most important to-dos in sight, the rest will fall into place.

So, obviously, we need to get those big rocks to fit in this vase, right? Let's approach it in a new way.

First, we fill the vase with the big rocks. Then we pour in the pebbles. They sprinkle over the big rocks and trickle down to the bottom of the vase. And finally, we pour in the sand. It fills in all the empty spaces around the big rocks and the pebbles. *It all fits.*

This is how we need to look at our priorities. We need to identify them, and we need to put them first.

I do this every day (well, almost every day . . . sometimes I get lazy or so busy I don't sit down and think about it, and that's never a good thing).

I set my intention. My Big Rock. My *one thing* that I need to accomplish that day.

Many days, I have several Big Rocks. But I pick one that I need to accomplish that day. If I do nothing else but address this one Big Rock, I can call my day a success.

Some days, it's as simple as going for a walk. Other days, like today, it was "finish new planner cover designs."

Once I get my Big Rock out of the way, the rest falls into place (and I often have time to get several Big Rocks in my vase every day, if I'm taking care of myself).

When we keep our most important to-dos in sight, the rest will fall into place.

At the end of the day, does it really matter if you got to check Facebook a fifth time? Nope, it doesn't. But if you had a work project due and it's going to be late because you got sucked into your Facebook feed, you're going to be feeling regret. And now you've thrown your next day off track, too, because

Setting my intention and focusing on that one thing until it's done is key to keeping my sanity.

you're going to have to hustle to get that project done.

Y'all. I'm the Queen of Procrastination. The Princess of the Last Minute. I've been this way my whole life.

I am not suggesting that I have it all together, or that I ever get anything done early (because I don't!). But I have learned that setting my intention and focusing on that one thing until it's done is key to keeping my sanity (and also, key to *gettin' thangs done*).

Setting my intention is easy. Literally, all I do is write it down in my planner, either the night before or when I sit down to work in the morning, depending on how organized I'm feeling. I write it in my planner, but you could set your intention in any way you choose. For some people, just mentally setting an intention is enough. You also might set phone notifications to remind yourself a few times a day to check in with your intention (I actually avoid using my phone when I can, but this can be a helpful tool).

I really love the word "intentional," and, as I've gotten older, I've learned that I need to be very intentional with my time, my energy, and my life. The busier my days get, the more conscious I have to be to slow them down and keep the focus on what really matters. I do this very intentionally by setting limits on what I bring into my life. I encourage you to spend a few moments each day thinking about how you can be intentional with your time.

Choose those Big Rocks wisely!

How to Plan

The first thing I want to tell you is this—whatever system works best for you is the system you should use. I'm going to share my personal system for managing my day-to-day life, work, and goals. I'll also show you a condensed version (although I try to keep it simple to begin with) and I'll show you some tips for getting even more in depth, if you are super detail-oriented.

I've also got a few life hacks (in the old days, we just called them "tips") that might help free up some extra time for you, so stay tuned for those, too (I'm all about working smarter, not harder).

I've included lots of fun planning pages for you to use, too. You can download more of these pages on my website, so you'll never run out!

I spend some time at the end of each month getting ready for the next month. I also sit down every Sunday to plan out my week, and spend just a few minutes each day planning out the next day. This sounds time consuming, I know, but it's something I actually love to do. And most important, it helps me reach my goals and get things done.

If these ideas don't resonate with you, just take what feels helpful and skip the rest.

Once a Month

Whenever I need to write something down in my planner, I put it on my monthly calendar. That goes for birthdays, parties, soccer games, vacations, deadlines, and every other thing I need to have on my calendar. This is why I like having a big calendar! I will often email myself dates I need to remember if they come up when I'm out and about (for example, if I make a playdate for one of my kids, there's a 99 percent chance I'll completely forget it, so I just shoot myself a quick email with the date). You might want to carry around a notebook for this, or put it in your phone's calendar. I like sending it to my email because I am an "inbox zero" girl and I know I'll see it in my inbox when I'm going through my emails and stick it in my planner. Also, we get a lot of communications from the school via email, so I am always transferring dates from my email to my planner. Again—you can totally use an app or digital calendar if you prefer, but I find that writing things down helps me connect with what I'm doing *and* it keeps me off my phone.

The last day of the month (if you miss it, it's no big deal—you can do it earlier, or a few days into the new month), I sit down with my planner and just spend some time checking in. I mostly use this time to go over goals and deadlines coming up, and I create a fun little vision board in my planner.

In my planner, there's a space at the top of every month to write out my goals and priorities. I use this space to designate a few things I want to work on. I'll write in quotes that are meaningful to me (or sometimes, just funny, because that's important, too) and I'll often pick a few words that I want to focus on in an intentional way (like, the word "intentional"—that is such an important word to me). I mostly decorate this space using planner stickers and my favorite pen. It doesn't have to be fancy, but this helps me give purpose to the month ahead. It also makes me excited about what I am going to be working on that month!

I've included a sample page here for you, so you can do the same. But you don't need this specific monthly calendar to do this exercise. You could easily do the same thing on an index card that you tuck in your purse, inside your journal, or on a blank piece of paper that you keep in your planner.

This is my way of keeping excited and inspired year-round (it's easy to be excited and inspired in January, but our enthusiasm tends to wane as the days get warmer).

If I have specific goals for that month, this is also when I try to write those down with some measurable action items that I can work on to complete them.

One thing I've learned about goals is to make them as measurable and specific as possible. If my goal for the year is to lose fifty pounds, I wouldn't make my goal for January to lose fifty pounds. I would make it something super attainable, like lose five pounds. It can be frustrating if you feel like you're always setting goals and not reaching them. Keeping your goals manageable and doable in the time frame you're given is key to staying on track.

Depending on how elaborate I want to get, this can take twenty minutes or hours.

To simplify this, just keep a monthly calendar nearby to jot down activities as they pop up. You might want to use your phone's calendar instead. You can import that information into a daily planner later, or work directly from your phone. It's totally up to you. The important thing is that you're tracking the important events and deadlines in your life. I've shared some examples in the pages that follow.

do what
you love
&

BE MINDFUL

follow your bliss

☑ Visit horse and
donkeys 3 times

5K training

IMPORTANT

TO DO
Black friday
prep work

this NOVE
holiday seas
→ learn calligra

Monday	Tuesday		Wednesday	Thursday	Friday
	31		1	2	3
7			8	9	10
14			15	16	17
21			22	23 thanksgiving → cowboys! Thanksgiving	24 black friday TODAY IS THE DAY
28 monday			29	30	1

Once a Week

Every Sunday, I pull out my planner, the pile of paper I've collected that week from my kids' school, any mail that needs to be dealt with, my favorite markers, and all my pretty planner stickers.

I flip back to my monthly calendar and import any important dates into the weekly calendar (soccer, lunch dates, work meetings, vet appointments, etc.). My monthly calendar is messy—I'm often writing things down in sloppy handwriting, with whatever pen I can find. I cross things out all the time as plans change. I jot notes in the margins. I really do not care what it looks like.

When I sit down with my weekly calendar, I take more care. I use my favorite pen and plug in all the activities for the week.

I also create a to-do list for that week. More often than not, it involves carrying over items from the to-do list from last week. Sometimes, I get so tired of writing the same things down every week, it motivates me to check them off my list.

I don't usually decorate my planner or make it pretty at this point. I like to leave it wide open for changes and keep it 100 percent functional. But I do often go back to the last week and fill in notes (how the weekend went, etc.). This is when I'll use my planner stickers and make the week look pretty (my goal is to have planners that are entirely functional, but also make fun keepsakes that the kids can look back on—they're full of notes and pictures, and very scrapbook-y).

I also use this time to go through the pile of flyers the kids brought home (many with dates I need to stick in the planner). If I need the flyer, I'll stick it in the pocket of my planner. This is where I keep everything that I collect randomly throughout the week that I need to address (like bills, or birthday party invitations).

Sketching out my week, which is really all you need to do, only takes me fifteen or twenty minutes. I spend a lot more time making it pretty.

Sunday is also when we meal plan (although we usually do that early in the day, and then go grocery shopping). If you're strapped for time, and you're not meal planning, it's time to start. This one simple thing can save you hours of time, tons of money, and I promise you, it will reduce the chaos in your life. Meal planning for LIFE, y'all!

I also use this time to take a look at what Monday is going to bring (see below for more on that).

> To make it even easier you can bypass the monthly calendar page completely, and just write in the activities on the appropriate days, or, again, use an app to track your schedule.

Every Day

Every night, I take a look at what I need to do the next day. Based on the day's activities, I set my intention for the day. Sometimes it's a word, like *focus* or *patience* or *hustle*. Other times, it's a goal—like *write two thousand words* or *yoga class*. And other times, it's something important that needs to be my priority for the day, like *Jack's birthday* or *product launch* or Outlander *premiere* (if nothing else, I have my priorities straight!).

I write this at the top of that day so I know how important it is.

Remember the Big Rocks analogy? This is exactly what that is: my Big Rock for the day.

Then, I write a to-do list. I keep it as short and manageable as possible. I've also learned to keep it realistic. We all have a to-do list a mile long. I keep that mile-long to-do list elsewhere. There is literally no way I'm going to organize my linen closet, prepare for the garage sale, and complete all of my work items. But I don't want to forget that I need to organize that linen closet and prepare for that garage sale. So, I keep those things on another list (I keep mine in the back of my planner—in the off chance I have free time, or on the days I decide to tackle big chores, I can always pull from it).

My daily to-do list contains the things I must do that day. Like, meal plan, or finish a blog post, or exercise, or stick a birthday present for my nephew in California in the mail. These are all tasks that I can realistically complete that day, and that I can cross off when they're complete.

If I have time, I'll jot down some notes about the prior day, if there is something I want to remember (like a movie we saw, or a book I finished).

This takes maybe five to ten minutes a day. I like to do this at night, so I know what's going on the next day (I've learned the hard way that it's important for me to check in with my planner so I know what's going on the next day—it's important to know if I need to prep something the night before, or wake up early the next day). If I don't get around to it at night, though, I just do it first thing in the morning.

Actually, I love to sit down at my desk and check in with my plans and to-do list for the day before I open my laptop or look at my phone. It's a more peaceful way to start the day than opening Facebook and seeing all the notifications yelling at me, or turning on my phone and seeing all the texts I need to deal with (I sleep with my phone in airplane mode so I don't get any notifications or calls when I'm trying to sleep—if this sounds appealing, but you need to have your phone on for emergencies, you can change your phone's settings to only allow calls or texts from certain people during designated hours).

This is super simple already and only takes a few minutes each day. Sometimes, you've got to put in the work, you know what I mean? But another option for your to-do list is to keep it in a notebook (this is helpful if you have an online planner, or if your planner doesn't have room for a to-do list every day). I used to have a big spiral notebook that I would write a to-do list in every day, carrying over anything from the previous day and adding new things as necessary. If you decide to just have one long-running to-do list like this, it's easy to miss things as the list grows. If you don't want to rewrite it every day—and who can blame you for that?—an option might be to have a weekly to-do list that you can add to during the week, but redo at the beginning of the next week.

I strongly recommend keeping your to-do list in a notebook or planner or online and sticking to that *one* to-do list. If you're using multiple notebooks or have paper scattered all over the house with lists all over them (raising my hand in shame, because I still have a tendency to do this), it can be really, really hard to keep up with it all and stay focused. Also, your husband might not know that the random envelope you grabbed from the mail stash had your Very Important To-Do List on it, and he might throw it away.

Just sayin'.

You can see how I structure my week below.

Checking in with Your Goals

But what about those goals? Those need love, too. When I create my goals with measurable action items, it becomes easy to incorporate them into my daily life.

Here's an example: if one of my goals is to write seven thousand words that week, I can put "write a thousand words" on my to-do list every day. Or, if I see one day is super busy, I can skip that day and write two thousand words the next day.

If my goal is to lose five pounds, and my action items are to follow a clean eating meal plan and exercise every day, those are items I can write down on my to-do list and cross off once they're complete. It feels so good to cross things off the to-do list!

I check in periodically with the action items and overall big picture of my goals to make sure I am staying on track.

I am often working on multiple goals simultaneously. Some of them are very long-term (write a book). Other are shorter (go to two yoga classes this week). Recording them all in one place helps me to keep track of what I'm working on, and breaking them down into smaller goals that I integrate into my every day helps me accomplish them.

Another tip for goal setting: Reward yourself when you meet your goals! These don't have to be big rewards, but they should be encouraging and meaningful.

I usually reward myself with donuts. Because donuts are meaningful, and nobody can convince me otherwise.

Project Planning, Prioritizing Your Priorities, and Balancing Multiple Responsibilities

I know we are all busy and have lots of things on our plates. This is where it can get tricky when we're trying to reach our goals and make things happen. If we feel overwhelmed by all the balls we're juggling, it can be really hard to step out from under everything and decide what to work on first.

When I started my job at the insurance firm, I was constantly in a state of overwhelm. After I'd been there just a few months, a coworker left for a long vacation and left me a list of things to work on while he was gone. Nothing weird about that.

But when I sat down and added that list to my existing list, I was completely overwhelmed. I was still so new that I didn't have a clear understanding of the relationships we had with each client. I didn't understand all the rules behind insurance deadlines. Every task seemed just as important as the next, and I didn't know where to start.

I asked my boss to help, and with her assistance, we went through the lists and determined what were immediate priorities, what could wait a few days, and what I could be working on in the background when I had time. It was such a relief to have this clear picture of my workload.

This serves as a lesson to ask for help when you need it, but it also reinforces the importance of understanding your priorities.

When we can define what we're working on, we can attack it harder.

I have lots of projects going on at the same time for work. And while I wish I could work on one thing at a time until it's done (and sometimes, it works out that I can), most of the time I need to be working on several things at once. *But never at the same time.*

Distractions will kill your productivity, and in turn, kill your goals.

What I mean by that is I that set time aside to work specifically on each project every day. I don't try to multitask, and go back and forth between writing a blog post and designing a new product. Rather, I sit down and give myself an hour to work on my blog post. Then I set aside a couple more hours for the product I'm trying to design. Some days, I dedicate the entire day to one project. Other days, I might touch four or five different projects.

This system works for any projects you're working on, be they home improvement, or work related, or even fitness related.

Put all of your energy into whatever it is you're working on, while you're working on it.

Distractions will kill your productivity, and in turn, kill your goals.

I'm sharing some examples of exactly how I do this on the next pages.

You'll see I've got each day broken down into six different boxes. These are the things I'm working on for the week. On the left-hand side of my page, I label the rows. You can see I've got my projects labeled book, conference, blog, website design, social media, and a product development. These are primarily the items I work on every single day, so these categories rarely change, but if your life is different from week to week, you would switch out the categories as necessary (as soon as I get my new website designed, I'll be removing the website category from my planner *and* checking off a major, long-term goal, too).

Every day, I write out the things I need do *that day* to keep these projects moving along. I will sometimes set mini goals for myself each week, too, that I make a note of here.

I cross off the items as I complete them.

This is also where I track deadlines and due dates.

I use this system for most of my work-related activities (if I'm required to go to a meeting or have a conference coming up, I also make sure to put it in my regular planner).

I can't tell you how much this has simplified my life. Every day, I can open to my schedule and see exactly what I need to accomplish. I still have to be flexible—things come up, and sometimes we have to move stuff around, and that's okay. At least I know exactly what I need to do when I sit down to work.

And that's really half the battle, right? Knowing where to start? People tell me all the time, "I just don't know where to start—it seems so overwhelming!"

I totally get that. It is overwhelming. Sometimes it can feel impossible, even. But when we break something huge into doable little pieces, we realize that it's actually not impossible. It's not that overwhelming. It's out there, waiting for us, and we just need to start moving toward it.

Last year, I went with my sister, my BFF, and a group of my sister's friends to Seattle for a bachelorette party. Because my BFF (Sara) and I were old and boring, we ended up going to bed earlier and getting up earlier than the rest of the girls (which is a far cry from my early days of travel that revolved around local bars, *not that there's anything wrong with that*). One morning, we found ourselves up bright and early and headed out to explore the Space Needle and the Chihuly Garden and Glass museum. If you're not familiar with Chihuly, google him real quick so we're on the same page here.

If you don't have Google nearby, here's the super quick rundown of Dale Chihuly. Dale Chihuly is an artist famous for his enormous glass blowing sculptures. They are truly incredible, and beautiful in a way I can't express with words.

So anyway, Sara and I went to the Chihuly museum and strolled through the exhibits and even braved the Seattle weather in February to meander through the outside displays. We were oohing and aahing over everything, and I marveled at the combination of artistic vision and logistics that had to go into creating these pieces (glass and fire can't be an easy medium to work with, right? I mean, I'd be breaking stuff left and right and probably burning myself a bunch, too).

Toward the end of our experience, we strolled into a theater where they were playing videos about Dale Chihuly and some of the projects he had worked on. One of the videos was about a display he did in Jerusalem.

At the time, my husband and I were really struggling with what to do about our printer. It was time to buy our own, but we were really uncertain, and the idea felt very overwhelming.

As I watched Dale Chihuly and his crew transport glass spikes longer than my car and a glass tree larger than my house across the world and then set them up again in the Citadel Tower, I heard him say something along the lines of, "We had no idea how we were ever going to make this work—it seemed impossible" (I'm paraphrasing there).

Hearing him admit his apprehension and then seeing his art in the Citadel Tower made me realize that we all have moments where it feels impossible. And yet, if we move forward, one step at a time, we are able to get it done. No job is too big, and no dream is too grand, when we apply ourselves.

Speaking of grand dreams, I was at the local coffee shop today and they had HGTV on—in this particular show, people were buying islands to live on, and I was like, *yes . . . I want an island!* So, I'll be adding that to my vision board, even though Charles told me I'd do horribly on an island because they don't have salads, and this might be true.

I don't actually know how Dale Chihuly executed his idea for filling the Citadel with colorful glass, but I'm guessing he had some processes in place and some logistics to work through. When I imagine the logistics behind moving large amounts of glass across the world and setting it up in Jerusalem, all of a sudden my logistics seem a lot more manageable.

You can see how I structure my weekly workload on page 133.

You can use the pages on the next spread to plan out your own week. Print out more copies by using the QR code below.

TO-DO			

THINGS TO DO	THINGS TO DO	THINGS TO DO	THINGS TO DO

SCHEDULE SCHEDULE SCHEDULE SCHEDULE

Why Is It So Easy to Get Derailed?

You *know* what your Best Life looks like. Or at the very least, you're on the path to clarifying it (you wouldn't have picked up this book if you weren't trying to make some changes or work on some personal growth, right?!).

So, why is it that our destination can be so clear, and our path so muddled?

Last year, I found myself tangled up in a huge web of stress and unease. It was the beginning of the holiday season, which is basically my favorite time of year, ever. I know the holidays are stressful for everyone, but I took it to another level, y'all.

We were launching a new product, I was running my website full-time, and were attending some large vendor events. We were also moving to a new headquarters (in December, because why not make the craziness as bad as possible?) and I was working on a huge update to an existing product. In addition to this, I was working with several brands to create content for their own holiday campaigns (to be featured on my website, which meant I was creating it all from scratch, for my readers).

And that was just work stuff! In December we have our anniversary, my birthday, my son's birthday, my mom's birthday, my sister's birthday, my sister's husband's birthday, Christmas, and our annual Christmas Eve party. It was too much.

I didn't realize what the stress was doing to me at the time, but *I was in a bad place.*

I couldn't fall asleep. I couldn't remember anything (my memory was literally slipping away, and it freaked me out.). I was irritable, and not in the "I'm kind of grumpy" kind of way. No, I was legit Rage-y with a capital "R." I was trying to eat well, but no matter what I did, I couldn't lose weight. I walked around with a heavy, swirly feeling in my head and a sinking feeling in my gut.

I didn't feel like myself, and that was terrifying.

Terrifying enough to see a doctor (and I never go to the doctor!).

I thrive on deadlines and getting things done, but in the process of taking care of all my obligations, I'd completely neglected to take care of *myself*.

I wanted to do all the things I was doing. I liked most of the projects I was working on. I was excited about the future and how everything I was doing was pushing us in the right direction.

But all of that? It was nothing when I felt like I was starting to crack. *How in the world could I hold everything else together when I couldn't even keep myself in one piece?*

I had made a common mistake. I let my priorities slip out of my vision. With my priorities tucked safely away out of sight, it was easy to justify working crazy hours on multiple projects without any help.

When I made the appointment with the doctor, I cried. I cried because I felt so far removed from my true self that I was hoping (seriously hoping!) that she'd tell me I had some crazy hormonal imbalance or weird health issue that was making me feel like this. I couldn't imagine any other reason to feel so out of whack—it had to be that something was terribly wrong with me.

At this point, I did what any self-respecting worrier would do. *I googled.* I read a ton of health books. I took quizzes. I self-diagnosed myself with about twelve different hormone disorders, and I started random supplements.

All in the name of health and finding the Old Me and bringing her back home.

Then, I went to the doctor. I told her my worries. This was a holistic doctor, and I knew she was hearing me loud and clear. We took bloodwork—not the typical blood panels that a "normal" doctor would take, but a full panel that tested for everything under the sun, and then some.

As I walked into her office to get the results, I just knew she was going to tell me that I had a thyroid issue that was making my brain short-circuit and food shovel itself spontaneously into my mouth.

The results, then, were shocking. In her words, "These are better than pretty much any results I ever see in here."

Y'ALL. My bloodwork said I was healthy as a horse.

She gave me some diet recommendations, told me to stay off my phone (like, put it in another room when I sleep, even), and gave me a couple of supplements to take home.

I was so disappointed!

The truth was, though, that I needed this reset. It was easy to blame something external for my health issues, but I was the one to blame. I had let myself fly off the rails under the burdens of stress and a hectic lifestyle that I had created myself.

Once I acknowledged that I had put myself in this situation, I realized that I could pull myself out of it.

We all get derailed now and then. How many times have you been on a healthy eating kick, only to have a donut one morning and then find yourself eating *allll the sugar* for days to come?

When we start working toward a goal, it's exciting and new and we feel inspired. Keeping up with that motivation and drive can be tough, though.

This is totally normal and you are not alone.

Finding support with others (in a supportive online group or with real-life friends, for example) can be a huge motivator when we're trying to stay on track. I've also learned that taking a day off every now and then to focus on my true priorities can help me reset.

It's easier than ever to get distracted (Facebook! Snapchat! The news!). We live in a world full of distractions. When you feel yourself drifting off course, take some time to reconnect with yourself and the people who support you. Check in with your vision boards and your goals and remember why it is you have those goals in the first place.

And then, get yourself back on track. You've got this.

TO-DO		monday 21	tuesday 22	wednesday 23
netflix post	book	· ~~2,000 words~~	· ~~2,000 words~~	· ~~2,000 words~~
vision boards				
~~hfalls~~				
candy corn refresh	pinners		· side hustle course outline	
hp post ?				
~~spirit giveaway~~				
september stationery	blog	· ~~theddars links~~ + invoice to Rachel · ~~multopia links~~ ~~to justin~~ · ~~hfalls post~~	→ invoice to rachel	→ ~~invoice to rachel~~ · netflix post
	website etc.	· ~~tailwind tribes~~ · ~~emails~~		· ~~emails~~
	social	· ~~CE group~~ · ~~boob groups~~ · ~~CE FB+IG~~ · ~~Shop FB+IG~~ · ~~hfalls post~~	- promote pinner - ~~hfalls social~~	· ~~promote pinner~~ · ~~answer IG comments~~ · CE FB+IG · Shop FB+IG · 21 DF group + FB · Budget group2
	product dev.	· MP weekly - xtra - covers 3 hrs	~~MP - 3 hours~~	· finish MP

When Goals Change

At the beginning of the year, I like to reflect on previous goals and take some time to create a vision board outlining some of the things I want to do in the coming year. This process is usually reflective of where I am *at that moment in my life*. We all know things can change, though, and this is where it's important to be flexible and realistic about our goals.

It's okay to change directions. It's okay to scrap a goal completely. We all change, and as we change, so do the things we want.

I've learned to check in every so often with my plans and dreams and see if they're still the same.

Sometimes, it turns out that I'm no longer interested in a particular goal. Or maybe my direction has changed. Or maybe a product I had high hopes for has flopped and I need to reevaluate. Or maybe my dream just feels kind of stale.

These are all signs that it's time to shake things up a bit.

It's okay to change directions. It's okay to scrap a goal completely. We all change, and as we change, so do the things we want. There's a difference between quitting something because we no longer want it and quitting something because we're giving up—and only you can decide what your motives are, and you'll know if you're abandoning ship because you really don't want to be there anymore or because you just don't like the work involved.

Here's the thing: reaching your goals is going to take work. It's going to get uncomfortable. We have to be prepared for some discomfort, and we have to be willing to work through it. But kind of like those uncomfortable yoga poses, it's worth it—there's something better waiting for us on the other side.

Other times, we have to be willing to make little tweaks to our goals.

I'll give you a real-life, real-time example. I'm currently working on next year's day planner, which is set to launch in just a few weeks. A couple of months ago, when time apparently must have felt unlimited, I decided that I wanted to redo the entire inner workings of the planner.

But then, life happened.

I got busy. Soccer started. It's busy season. We have lots and lots and lots of things going on right now. A few nights ago, I sat in my office with some Neil Diamond playing in the background (he can still rock it), struggling over the new planner layout. I had an idea for what I wanted, but the vision in my head wasn't translating onto paper like I expected. For hours, I played with the design—moving this, moving that, tweaking a color and then changing it back again.

It just wasn't working, and I realized, late at night, that I had two choices—try to force something and push back production even more, or let it be and move forward with what I already had.

In this case, after balancing all the other to-do items I had going on in my head, I chose to let it be.

Instead of making drastic changes to the current design, I settled on freshening up the colors. An entire planner refresh, with everything else I have going on, just wasn't going to work

I was disappointed for, like, five seconds.

But it was also very freeing. I would get the planner made. The current design is fine. And all of a sudden, I had several hours' less work on my plate.

I am constantly making little tweaks and redirects to my goals and my plans as my circumstances change. That doesn't mean I lose sight of the prize—it means that I am constantly changing course as necessary to reach my final destination.

If you're hiking down a cool mountain trail and halfway to your picnic spot, you come upon a log across the trail, you wouldn't turn around and go back. You'd assess the situation and make a judgment call about what to do next. Most likely, you'd go over it, under it, or around it. If you had the tools I suppose you could also chop through it with the axe you're carrying, thus paving the way for everyone behind you, too. And maybe you could even take the scrap wood home with you to use as firewood or build a cabin or something (wow, that metaphor really worked for me there).

You see what I mean, though. Sometimes, we have to deviate from our plans and that is totally normal and totally okay.

In fact, this ability to be flexible and bend with the changing winds keeps you strong.

I struggle with being flexible. In some areas, I'm the most flexible person imaginable (you should see what passes for dinner or a clean house on some days). But in other areas of my life, I'm a super perfectionist. I've learned that while it's hard to let go of my detail-oriented, control-freaky, *it-must-be-exactly-so* tendencies, it's also really important.

That's not to say you need to slack off or turn over control of everything you love. It just means that we could all benefit from learning to go with the flow a bit.

When I was in my late teens and early twenties, I worked every summer in the horse exhibit at our county fair (which was a huge county fair). Every year, I helped my friend who ran the 4-H horse show. Among other things, I would usually check everyone in during the morning of the fair and help direct them to their stalls. There would usually be large groups coming to this show, and it was important that their horses all be stabled together.

One cool June morning, I was checking in a large group when I noticed a mistake on the stall chart. The horses were split up. This happened every now and then, and I was always able to shuffle things around and make it work. This particular group was so large, though, that I couldn't make it work.

I analyzed the chart six ways from Sunday and no matter what I did, I couldn't make it happen. Meanwhile, the 4-H leader was getting louder and grumpier. "I brought all these kids and we're sharing a tack room and we need to be together," she said. More than once. I was getting flustered under her quickly mounting anger, and I was frustrated that I couldn't make this work.

If something's not working, change it.

"I'll be right back," I told her, and I took my chart to the boss.

She took one look at it and said, "Just tell her she has to put some horses on the other side, and there's nothing we can do about. It's no big deal."

"But I feel like we can make it work," I said.

"Look," she told me. "I know you want it to be perfect. But we need to keep things moving and get these horses stabled, and it's not that big of a deal."

That was a pivotal moment for me, because, until then, I hadn't actively realized that I actually did want things to be perfect. I prided myself on my "go with the flow" mentality, but actually, I was kind of a perfectionist about some things. Like, horse stalls, for example.

I took a deep breath. I returned to the angry 4-H leader. I explained that there was a mistake, I was sincerely very sorry, but that we needed to put a couple of horses in another location due to my mistake.

This was a learning lesson that just kept on giving.

The 4-H leader took it in stride. She was fine. The horses were fine. The kids who had to walk thirty extra feet to their tack room were fine. Ultimately, it really wasn't a big deal—and definitely wasn't worth stressing over.

It's important to be open to change and to be willing to chart that new territory as obstacles arise. Sometimes we can anticipate these changes in advance (and for someone like me, that's always ideal—I really hate it when things change on me unexpectedly).

Other times, though, change pops up unexpectedly and we need to roll with it or risk getting stuck.

If something's not working, *change it*.

If you had big plans to start a new business but life threw you a curveball and the timing is no longer right, take a deep breath and reevaluate your situation. We all have things like that happen to us, and it doesn't mean you'll never open your business. It just means you need to rethink your plan of attack or, possibly, wait out this season of your life until the timing is right. The older I get, the easier that is to say. We don't need to kid ourselves that we can do it all, and when we keep our priorities clear in our line of vision, it's easier to make important decisions like this.

I want to encourage you to check in with your goals, your vision boards, and your plans every few months. For most of us, checking in a few times a year is all we need. If you're working on something super specific with tons of moving pieces, you might want to check in monthly or even weekly until you've reached your goal.

Here are some questions to ask yourself:

- What is my goal?

- Has my goal changed?

- Have my circumstances changed?

- Do I have an action plan in place?

- Have I been consistent?

- If consistency has been a problem, why is that? What do I need to change to be consistent?

- As I work toward this goal, what's working for me?

- What's not working for me?

On Failure and Feeling Like a Fraud

Have y'all heard of Impostor Syndrome?

Wikipedia defines it as, "a concept describing individuals who are marked by an inability to internalize their accomplishments and a persistent fear of being exposed as a 'fraud.'"

I think we all have a little bit of Impostor Syndrome inside us. It's that annoying little voice telling you, "Who do you think you are?" when you try to do something new. It's the voice that reminds us, "Everyone is going to think your idea is so lame!" when you want to put something new out there. It's the little tug we feel in our throats when we envision our failures before they've even happened.

Guys. I am the same way.

Five minutes ago, I got off the phone with Charles.

"I just feel so stuck!" I whined. "I am writing this book, and I'm literally not an expert on anything."

Now, if I sit back and think about it, this isn't entirely true. I'm an expert on horses. I am an expert at blogging. I would even say I'm an expert at creating a job for myself out of nowhere and turning it into a full-time business that supports my family. I am an expert at planning, and I'm pretty good at making things happen.

But in that moment, as the words for this book felt choked off from the page, as I stared at my pile of note cards, all out of order and strewn across my already cluttered desk, and as I looked at the deadline looming nearer and nearer, I felt like a fraud. A total author wannabe. A waster of my own time. A person people would never take seriously, because, *who the heck am I, anyway*?

So, I let myself wallow in a Pity Party for One. I checked Instagram (again). I made my dog abandon his warm

That resistance you sometimes feel, the urge to just throw in the towel rather than creep outside the comfortable little protective bubbles we've all built around ourselves, is totally normal. But you can work through it.

spot on the couch and come sit by me so I could scratch his ears. I walked aimlessly around the house and felt sorry for myself, because *what had I got myself into*?

Unfortunately, though, books don't write themselves. After I stopped feeling sorry for myself and realized that I was just being a whiny chicken who was afraid to fail (coming down from a caffeine high at the same time!), I pulled it together enough to get back to the task at hand. I also realized that I wanted to write a book, that I had brought this "stress" on myself, and that I could choose to be stressed or move forward joyfully with the task at hand.

Here's the thing. It's really, really, *really* easy to quit (unless you're quitting caffeine, which I am here to tell you is not easy to quit, nor is it any fun, but that's a different story for a different day). It's easy to give up.

It's normal to feel like a failure or a total loser, especially when we step outside our comfort zone.

That resistance you sometimes feel, the urge to just throw in the towel rather than creep outside the comfortable little protective bubbles we've all built around ourselves, is totally normal. But you can work through it.

Part of this comes from having confidence in yourself. I know, I know—it sounds so clichéd, but if you can't believe in yourself, you can't expect others to, either.

Use those affirmations. Use those positive labels.

Fake it till you make it, y'all.

I believe the thing that keeps us from following our biggest dreams is not lack of resources, but fear. We're afraid of finally getting what we really want.

Or, we're afraid of all the steps we have to go through to get there. We're afraid of putting ourselves out there and being laughed at. We're afraid of picking up the phone and calling strangers who might be able to help. We're afraid of being laughed at, of being judged, of being Internet famous for tripping onstage.

Rather than put ourselves out there, we crawl into our safe little shells and live our safe little lives just like we think we're supposed to.

We stifle the truest pieces of ourselves so that we can conform and fly under the radar.

And in doing so, we miss out. *On a lot.*

It takes a lot of courage to share our stories. It takes bravery to quit a job and start your own company. It takes nerve to ask your boss for a raise, and it takes serious effort (and literal sweat!) to meet your healthy living goals.

And we are going to fail. We are going to fail so many times that even the thought of it can be enough to stop you in your tracks.

You know how I try to look at failures? I think of them as learning lessons.

I get really nervous when I launch a new product. I'm afraid nobody will buy it. That someone will tell me it's dumb, or worse, buy it and hate it and spew their venom across the Internet. I'm afraid we'll invest a bunch of money into it, I'll spend hours photographing it and getting it listed, and it will be a complete dud.

And sometimes, those things do happen (well, I've been lucky to avoid the Venom-Spewing Buyers Remorseful People of the Internet, but I'm sure that's coming, too!). You know what I've found, though? It's not really a big deal.

We've learned to dip our toe in the waters with new products, rather than launch ourselves all in. The amount of time that goes into creating a product is the same, whether we sell one or one thousand. So, of course, I always want to sell one thousand. But we start somewhere in between (a lesson we've learned the hard way).

Let me tell you about the mugs.

Cute mugs are everywhere. They're literally everywhere. They're in my grocery store, they're in my Instagram feed, they're in my cabinet. They're also not super expensive to buy, if you buy enough of them.

So when I decided we'd sell mugs, without thinking about the logistics (they're awkward to pack, they take up a lot of space, and they are waaaay easy to break), we made sure to buy enough of them to keep the costs down.

Before we knew it, we had hundreds of mugs that we needed to store. But it was okay! They were super cute and *everyone* was going to buy one. I took pictures, listed them online, shared them on social media, and waited for the orders to pour in.

And waited, and waited, and waited some more.

The mugs weren't selling. Every now and then, someone would come along and buy one, but mug sales were so sporadic that we'd do a little happy dance

when an order came through, and then be sad again as our Ginormous Stack o' Mugs stayed just as ginormous.

Eventually, we gave the mugs away at a conference. But not before we packaged all 350 in pretty tissue and tucked them safely into boxes. All 350 of them.

They were a total flop. Unless you were at the conference, *in which case they were a huge hit.* Everyone who got one loved them, and I still have people tagging me on social media with pictures of their mugs.

I took that failure and learned from it. Specifically,

- I'm not supposed to be in the mug business.

- It's okay to repurpose your plans (they made great gifts).

Even though it was a financial failure, and also took up a lot of space (both physically and in my brain, too, as we tried to get creative and move those mugs), in the end it was all okay and just one more small business learning lesson.

When we put ourselves out there, it can be hard. Being vulnerable is hard. Being open to criticism is hard. But when we let fear wrangle us in, we never realize our full potential. If you're too scared to accept that job interview because you think you might bomb it, or you feel underqualified, you will literally never get that job.

There has to be some discomfort to grow.

Did you have growing pains as a kid? When my own kids wake up in the middle of the night crying with pain in their legs, it's so easy for me to say, "It's just growing pains, you'll be fine." But the truth is, they hurt. Would I ask that they stop growing, though? Of course not. And not just because I need someone to mow my lawn ten years from now, either.

We all need to grow.

Every day, I share blog posts and create products and put them out there for the world to see. I'd by lying if I told you I have a thick skin. The opposite is true. I'm actually a super sensitive introvert whose day can be ruined by even the tiniest bit of snark in a comment directed my way. A mediocre review of one of my products can make my head swim in distress. My comfort zone is about as big around as I am, while my protective bubble stretches to encompass the entire house I sit in.

But I still put myself out there, every day, stretching well outside my personal limits. If I didn't do these things, I'd be sitting inside with a stack of books by my side for the rest of my life (although, not gonna lie, *that sounds pretty okay to me*).

I've developed some tools to help me be vulnerable and put myself out there. If you're struggling with feeling like a fraud or if fear of failure is crippling you, give this thought process a try.

What you put out there—the things you create, the work you accomplish, the goals you meet, is a gift. It is a gift to you, and it is a gift to other people. If other people don't like the gift, it's okay. You've given it as a gift, and everyone has the right to not like a gift.

If you create something, or make a change in yourself, and other people don't like it—it doesn't matter, because it wasn't for them. What you create, and the changes you make, are for people who appreciate them. When I watch a YouTube video with one of my products and read the comments, only to find someone griping about the price, I take a deep breath and remember that *I did not make this product for that person.* I made it for the person who is okay with the price and who finds value in the product. The person complaining about the price is wasting their time and energy, not mine, because it's not for them.

It's also important to remember that we all—*all of us*—have highs and lows. We have to ride out these cycles. I truly believe that slow and steady wins the race. One foot in front of the other.

This isn't to say it's always easy. I get queasy just thinking about putting myself in an uncomfortable situation. But every time I stretch outside of my comfort zone, I grow. Every time I embrace the fear butterflies swarming in my stomach before I do Something Big and move forward and complete the task at hand (horrifying as it might seem), I grow.

Fake it till you make it.

What Next?

I love the resources we have available to us in this day and age. Want to learn about something? It's at our fingertips. Want to take a class? Choose from thousands available online and take them from the comfort of your own home. Want to start a business, or lose weight, or take a really cool trip? Literally all of the resources are available to us, for free.

But what I've learned is that no matter how easy it becomes to get things or to learn more stuff in this digital age, one thing will always ring true when it comes to reaching our goals and living the lives of which we dream: we have to work hard.

I'm not afraid of hard work and I'm guessing that you're not, either. There's nothing worse than spinning your wheels on a project, though, and feeling like you aren't getting anywhere. That's why I truly believe we need more than just good ideas and a strong work ethic. We need ways to implement that work ethic!

When we identify our goals, visualize our success, and implement planning strategies that help us reach those goals, *we can make anything happen.*

I'd love to hear about your successes, your questions, and your ideas. Please come join us in our Make Anything Happen Facebook group, where we're keeping the conversation going.

GOAL:

GOAL PLAN:

DUE DATE:

Action Items:

_____

_____

_____

_____

_____

_____

_____

_____

_____

_____

_____

_____

_____

_____

_____

_____

_____

_____

_____

_____

_____

_____

_____

_____

_____

_____

_____

DREAM BIG
Notes, Ideas, Thoughts & More

GOAL COMPLETE

GOAL:

GOAL PLAN:

DUE DATE:

Action Items:

_____
_____
_____
_____
_____
_____
_____
_____
_____
_____
_____
_____
_____
_____
_____
_____
_____
_____
_____
_____
_____
_____
_____
_____
_____
_____
_____
_____
_____
_____
_____
_____

DREAM BIG
Notes, Ideas, Thoughts & More

GOAL COMPLETE

Use these pages to map out your vision board concepts.

Fill these pages with your favorite positive affirmations.

Let words inspire you! Use this space to write down your favorite quotes and words that you love.